THE RUNAWAY SCHOOLGIRL

THE RUNAWAY SCHOOLGIRL

THIS IS THE TRUE STORY OF MY DAUGHTER'S ABDUCTION BY HER TEACHER JEREMY FORREST

DAVINA WILLIAMS

JOHN BLAKE

Published by John Blake Publishing Ltd,
3 Bramber Court, 2 Bramber Road,
London W14 9PB, England

www.johnblakepublishing.co.uk

www.facebook.com/johnblakebooks 🄵

twitter.com/jblakebooks 🅃

This edition published in 2015

ISBN: 978 1 78418 120 8

British Library Cataloguing-in-Publication Data:

A catalogue record for this book is available from the British Library.

Design by www.envydesign.co.uk

Printed in Great Britain by CPI Group (UK) Ltd

3 5 7 9 10 8 6 4 2

Papers used by John Blake Publishing are natural, recyclable products made
from wood grown in sustainable forests. The manufacturing processes
conform to the environmental regulations of the country of origin.

Every attempt has been made to contact the relevant copyright-holders,
but some were unobtainable. We would be grateful if the
appropriate people could contact us.

This book is dedicated to all of my children.
I love you and I am so very proud of you.

CONTENT

CONTENTS

PREFACE

'She said they wanted privacy, that her family just wanted to be allowed to get on with their lives. So why is the mother of the Runaway Schoolgirl writing a book? She's just cashing in on what happened to her daughter ...'

I know that I'm going to receive a lot of criticism for writing this book, but it was something that I felt I needed to do. My friends and family have always been incredibly supportive and have never once not respected my wishes not to contact the press, but now I feel that the time is right for me to give my side of the story.

Rest assured, I am not doing it for the money. If it was money I was after, I would have taken up one of the six-figure deals that was offered to me when my daughter disappeared.

Hopefully this book will put the record straight about how

it feels to have your teenage daughter stolen from you. She had just turned fifteen; he was twice her age and knew he was breaking the law. Let me ask you, if you had a daughter, would you let her teacher do this to her?

Now it's my turn to tell you exactly what happened.

UNDER S. 1(1) OF THE SEXUAL OFFENCES (AMENDMENT) ACT 1992, WHICH PROVIDES ANONYMITY FROM PUBLICATION TO THE VICTIMS OF SEXUAL CRIME 'DURING THAT PERSON'S LIFETIME', SOME NAMES HAVE BEEN CHANGED TO PROTECT THE INNOCENT. IN SOME CASES, PSEUDONYMS USED BY THE PRESS REPLACE REAL NAMES.

PART ONE

TORN APART

CHAPTER 1

FRIDAY, 21 SEPTEMBER 2012

It was just a normal day. My eighteen-year-old son Lee was at work with my partner Paul and my fifteen-year-old daughter Gemma was at school. My four-year-old, Alfie, was at nursery and my baby daughter Lilly was having a morning nap. I was sitting at the kitchen table, flicking through the Argos catalogue looking for furniture for the new house. We hadn't found the right place yet, but with four children at home and my middle daughter Maddie, who was eleven, staying at her dad Max's place, we needed more space.

I was looking at bedroom furniture for Gemma when I received a text message from her school telling me that she hadn't turned up for registration that morning. There was a number to call or I could text a reply.

I knew I shouldn't have let her go to her friend Louise's for a sleepover on a school night, I thought. Gemma had pleaded with me to let her go, as Louise's dad was working late and she didn't want to be on her own. 'Just this once,' I told her, 'but make sure you get up for school in time. I don't want any phone calls saying you two haven't turned up!'

They were good girls. I didn't want them to be up all night chatting and then sleep through their alarm the next day, but I felt I could trust them.

I wasn't overly alarmed when I saw the text from the school. I knew they weren't playing truant – they never had, it just wasn't their thing. I sent a text straight back, asking them to confirm if Gemma hadn't been marked in for her first lesson.

Nearly an hour later, I received another text saying, 'Gemma is still showing absent', and I got straight on the phone to the school and asked the secretary to find out if Louise knew where Gemma was. I told her I would hang on while she went to check. In the back of my mind, an alarm bell rang. I sensed that something wasn't quite right, but I tried to dismiss it. It was probably a mistake, I told myself, Gemma would be in a different lesson.

After what seemed like hours, the school secretary came back on the phone, saying that Louise had told her that Gemma hadn't stayed at hers after all. Gemma had said that she was feeling unwell and had gone back home.

All of a sudden the alarm bells in my head got louder. I told the secretary that Gemma hadn't come home the night before. She went very quiet. After a short while, she spoke: 'I think you should call the police …'

I remember looking at my phone and, as I dialled 999, thinking this isn't happening to me. When I heard the voice at the other end of the line I had to concentrate on every syllable. 'My daugh-ter is miss-ing …' It felt like an out-of-body

3

experience, as if it wasn't me who was forming the words. It was like I was behind glass, looking at myself making the call. I can't remember exactly what the operator said to me, but the gist of it was that they were going to send someone over to the house.

I called Paul, Mum and my sister Charlotte, and told them that Gemma was missing. They all said they would be on their way.

I didn't know what to do with myself, so I went up to Gemma's bedroom. Already I had been in her room that day to measure up for furniture and I remember cursing her for the state it was in – drawers pulled out, clothes everywhere, your typical messy teenager.

I tried to kid myself that maybe she had been there all along, hiding under her bed or in a wardrobe, like it was just a silly game of hide and seek. I ripped off the duvet, looked under the bed and even heaved up the mattress, trying to convince myself she was somehow hiding there. I know it was ridiculous, but my mind was all over the place.

Random ideas started swimming around my head. What if Gemma had got back home late and couldn't get in? Maybe she had climbed over the garden fence and was asleep in the shed? The shed was packed full of junk, but could she have squeezed in somewhere? I ran to the end of the garden and checked it. I knew it was stupid, but I had to rule out every-where, even daft places like small cupboards that she couldn't possibly fit into.

I put up a message on my Facebook page: 'Has anyone seen my Gemma?' I got lots of replies asking for more details, but I only wanted to be told one thing – that someone knew where she was.

I just wanted to know she was somewhere safe. I called her friends Louise and Ben over and over again to find out if they knew anything, but I never got through. I felt like a zombie. 'Gemma doesn't like the dark,' I couldn't stop thinking. 'I hope she's not scared ...'

Finally, I went out to the front of the house and stood in the driveway. I just didn't want to be inside. 'If I'm not in there, then this isn't happening,' I thought. Mum, Charlotte, Paul and Lee arrived, and eventually they convinced me to go back indoors. Then we waited for what seemed like an eternity for the police to turn up. I think by this time I was in shock; I just couldn't function. I wasn't thinking the worst – that maybe she had been in an accident or attacked – because I wasn't thinking anything at all. I was totally numb.

Charlotte called Max, my ex. When he arrived, he, Charlotte and Lee went on Twitter and other social networking sites to spread the message further. Lee then went out with a group of friends in a car, searching the streets looking for Gemma and contacted everyone he knew, but he came back beaten and desperate that nobody had any news. Meanwhile, Mum and Charlotte went over to the school to see if they had any more information, but left with nothing more than the offer of a cup of tea and a prayer.

Paul and I were racking our brains about who Gemma could possibly be with, and I sent a text to Gemma's friend Ben to see if he knew anything. He eventually replied, saying: 'The only thing she said to me at school was that she didn't want to be here, but I thought it was just because of the rumours. Me and Louise are her only close friends and we don't know where she could have gone because she didn't mention anything.'

I knew what he meant about the rumours – there had

been some gossip involving Gemma and one of her teachers that had been doing the rounds, but I had dismissed it at the time.

Then two policemen turned up at the house and started asking the standard 'missing person' questions. 'What's her full name?' 'Her date of birth?' 'When did you last see her?' 'What's the name of her doctor and dentist?' I didn't really understand that last question at the time, but I later realised they were thinking that, if their worst fears were to come true, they would need Gemma's medical records to identify her body.

One of the officers asked me if Gemma and I had rowed before she disappeared, or if there was any reason why she may have had to run away, and it was then that the penny dropped. I remember thinking, 'Oh my God, they think I've killed her! They actually think I have killed my own daughter.' Of course I know now that they were only doing their job, but I couldn't take it all in at the time.

I felt like I was going mad. I couldn't believe this was happening to me.

The police then asked if Gemma's passport was missing – and, of course, when we went to check it wasn't in the usual place where we keep it. Two more officers from CID then arrived as the other two left and took a statement from me so that they could conduct a full police search. They also took one of my favourite school photos of Gemma in her Year 10 uniform. This was the picture that would later be splashed all over the newspapers throughout the following weeks.

I remember thinking: 'This is silly, she'll be home at 5pm. She's always home by then.' Then, just before 5pm, there was a knock on the door and two more police officers were standing there. I recognised one of them as he was assigned to Gemma's school and was also one of Max's colleagues.

He looked me in the eye. 'We need you to sit down,' he said. 'We know who she's with.'

CHAPTER 2

SIX MONTHS EARLIER

In March 2012 I received a phone call out of the blue from Miss Shackleton, who was the deputy head at Gemma's school, Kennedy High School in Eastbourne. She was also head of child safeguarding at the school, and it was in this capacity that she was contacting me.

She told me that Gemma had recently confided in a teacher that she was bulimic and had been self-harming. My first reaction was one of total disbelief: Gemma didn't have any problems with eating and was totally healthy. As for cutting herself, that was just ridiculous. Gemma never made any attempt to hide her body from me and, anyway, surely I would have noticed if she had any marks on her? Gemma and I have always been really close and she would have told me if she was upset about anything. She just wasn't that kind of girl.

I assured Miss Shackleton that I would make an appointment for Gemma to have a check-up with the doctor and talk everything through with her. I accepted the fact that my daughter might have wanted to talk to a teacher as she was under so much pressure to do well in her GCSEs. I could understand that she might have been struggling with all the extra tuition, as the school had such high expectations of her, but surely the idea of bulimia and self-harming was a misunderstanding?

During the conversation Miss Shackleton also mentioned that Gemma had been seen holding hands with Mr Forrest, the teacher in whom she had confided, on the flight home from a school trip to America in February. My first thought was that, like me, Gemma is terrified of flying and perhaps Mr Forrest had been trying to calm her down, but I wasn't happy about the idea of a teacher holding hands with my daughter. I pressed Miss Shackleton, but she told me it wasn't anything to be concerned about. She said she had already investigated and reassured me that it was nothing more than a supportive gesture during the flight. She just wanted me to know that the matter was in hand and that all was well; there was nothing untoward to be worried about.

When Gemma returned home from school that night I sat her down and we had a long talk. She told me that there had been stupid rumours going round about Mr Forrest holding her hand, but that it was just because she was so scared of flying, and she insisted that the self-harming thing was ridiculous. As for the bulimia, well, yes, she had been sick at school, she admitted, but it had been because she was so worried about getting through her exams.

I told her that she shouldn't put pressure on herself; if she didn't get the results she was aiming for, she would always have the option of doing re-takes at college. I didn't want her to become ill for the sake of her GCSEs and I also wanted her to understand that she wasn't under any pressure from anyone at home to get results. In my opinion, Kennedy High School was way too demanding. Instead of inspiring the pupils, the school just put them under huge amounts of stress.

Gemma and I hugged each other and during the weeks that followed we were closer than ever. She duly went along to see the doctor, who confirmed that physically she was perfectly healthy, and the whole drama seemed to blow over. Nonetheless, over the next few weeks, I made sure to look out for any telltale signs of an eating disorder, and I asked the older members of the family to be watchful and let me know if they thought Gemma was ever acting out of character. I wanted to keep a close eye on her, so I reminded her to make sure that she carried on texting me regularly when she wasn't at home. On one occasion, when Paul and I were visiting his family in Somerset and Gemma was staying with her nan, I virtually had hourly updates from her, telling me everything was fine.

Around three months after that first call from Miss Shackleton, on 11 June 2012, I gave birth to my beautiful baby daughter Lilly by C-section. On the same day, Miss Shackleton phoned again, but this time the call went to voicemail. There were a few complications with Lilly's birth and so it would be another three days before I was able to get back to her, and I left her a message with the receptionist. I asked Gemma if there was anything I needed to know, but she assured me there was nothing to worry about. I wondered if it was simply a courtesy call to check everything was back on track.

Miss Shackleton and I then played a bit of phone tennis.

When she didn't get back to me I just assumed everything was fine now.

How wrong I was …

CHAPTER 3

SUMMER HOLIDAYS

Towards the end of July, around a week before the school was due to break up for the summer holidays, I received a phone call from Mr Forrest, Gemma's teacher.

He was absolutely distraught. 'Some of the pupils are spreading rumours that I am having a relationship with Gemma and it's ruining my life,' he told me. When people asked Gemma if there was any truth in the story, he added, she neither denied nor confirmed it, and it had now got to the stage where it was affecting his relationship with his wife. He was sorry to put me in a difficult position, he said, but something had to be done about it as Gemma was, as he put it, being 'a bit of a pain'.

His voice was shaking to begin with, but he wasn't stumbling over his words. It was almost as if he had a script in front of him. But then he broke down and sobbed down the phone.

'You have to quash this rumour,' he pleaded. 'It just can't go on, it will destroy my career. It must be sorted out by the time we come back in September.'

Mr Forrest told me that he had been trying to support Gemma with her bulimia and self-harm issues, but that was the full extent of their relationship. It was just a teenage crush that had got out of hand.

I was gob-smacked. I was so angry, I couldn't believe what I was hearing and felt sick with shock. And yet from the tone of Mr Forrest's voice, I couldn't help but feel that he was telling the truth. He sounded so sincere, honest and vulnerable, and I felt so ashamed that Gemma could have behaved in this way. I assured him that I would deal with her and make sure the rumour was stopped once and for all. I've always brought up my children to respect other people and I was furious that matters were getting out of hand.

By the time Gemma arrived home later that day, Mr Forrest's words had been festering in my mind and I had wound myself up into a total fury. The moment she stepped through the front door, I tore her head off. 'How dare you spread rumours of a romance between you and Mr Forrest! I've had him sobbing on the phone to me. Don't you realise this could destroy his career and his family?'

Faced with this barrage of accusations, Gemma burst into tears and started defending herself. 'It's all lies,' she sobbed. 'It's everyone at school making things up, not me.' I kept pushing her. 'Why did he ring me then? There must be more to it than you say.' But Gemma was adamant that she was the injured party. She was stuck in the middle of the rumours, and was really upset and angry with me that I didn't believe her.

But I was angrier than I'd ever been before. I have always tried my best with my children and I felt ashamed that I had obviously not done a good enough job as a mother.

It was a horrific scene, and one that I regret to this day. I can't help thinking if only I had reacted differently and calmly, talked things through with Gemma, she might have opened up to me about what was really happening. As we all know, though, 20:20 hindsight is always easy.

After lots of tears and screamed accusations we both eventually calmed down. Gemma promised me that she would confront the people who were spreading gossip and tell them to stop telling lies. The summer holidays were coming up and she was determined to get everything back on an even keel so that it could all be forgotten by the time the new term began in September. I believed that she would do the right thing and so we agreed to say no more about it.

For the remaining days at school everything went back to normal. Soon after, the summer holidays began, and we all looked forward to being home together as a family and getting to know baby Lilly. Money was a bit tight as we were saving to move, so we didn't go abroad for a big holiday but spent a few days in Somerset with Paul's family. We had a couple of day trips to the zoo and park, Gemma often went off to see her nan and all the kids had friends round for barbecues and things like that.

Gemma and her friends Louise and Ben hung out a lot together, going to the beach, the local shopping centre and so on, just like any other fifteen-year-olds, but I always insisted that she regularly texted me to let me know where she was and when she would be back home. She would sometimes stay over at Louise's – they were practically living in each other's pockets at the time – and everything seemed to be back to normal after all the upset before the holidays.

I was still on maternity leave and was at home most of the time, so I would have known if there was anything untoward going on, wouldn't I?

CHAPTER 4

BACK TO SCHOOL

All too quickly, the summer was over. I vividly remember the day Gemma went off to school in her new Year 11 uniform. It was different to the normal uniform, as kids in the year choose what colour polo top they wear; in 2012, they chose deep blue. I remember thinking how grown-up Gemma looked as she went off on her first day back. Even so, she was still my 'little mermaid'. The first of my three daughters, she would always be my little girl.

When Gemma was tiny, I used to dress her up in frilly dresses, but when she grew up she didn't dress as a 'girly' teenager at all. She was never one of those teenagers who hitched up her school skirt into a mini or wore too much make-up. In fact, if anything, she would dress down with flat shoes, dark eyeliner and quite 'indie' clothes. She never tried to look or act older than she was.

With exams looming, it was important that Gemma knuckled down. All the early indications were that she was getting to grips with the new term, and it seemed all of the rumours about her and Mr Forrest had been forgotten. Every day when she got home from school, I would ask how her day had been, and every day she would tell me, 'Yes, everything's fine.'

Unfortunately, on Wednesday, 19 September, two days before Gemma was to go missing, I was to discover that everything had been far from fine.

I was busy running around attending to Lilly and Alfie when there was a knock on the door. There on the doorstep were an official-looking man and a woman. They looked at me very seriously and showed me their ID cards. Instantly I felt physically sick and started shaking. 'My name is Detective Constable Pawson,' said the man, 'and this is my colleague, who's a social worker. We would like to speak to you about your daughter Gemma.'

Of course I immediately thought the worst had happened and they were going to tell me that Gemma had been involved in an accident or something. I panicked and told them I wouldn't let them in until they told me the reason they were there. Now I know it sounds weird, but I thought everything would be all right so long as I could keep them outside; I felt safe in my space. I wasn't going to budge until they told me why they were there.

'We need to talk to you about a relationship your daughter Gemma may have been having with her teacher, Mr Jeremy Forrest.'

I have always been nervous about letting strangers into my house without really preparing myself; it is an insecurity of mine – I am very house proud and don't like things to be out of place. At that point, though, I let them in, relieved that it was just about those stupid rumours, safe in the knowledge that I would be able to put the record straight. I told them that I had already spoken to Mr Forrest and it was all lies, just tittle-tattle put around by school kids, and that I had also spoken to Gemma about it. There was nothing to be concerned about.

The next thing DC Pawson said hit me like a ton of bricks.

'Gemma is believed to have indecent pictures of Mr Forrest on her phone and we need to speak to you both about it.'

I couldn't believe what I was hearing and so I phoned Gemma straight away, trying to keep calm. 'Hi darling, where are you?' I said breezily. 'When will you be home?' Gemma could obviously tell from my voice that something wasn't right. 'I'm at school, Mum, what's the matter? You're scaring me.' I pulled myself together and tried to sound as normal as possible: 'No, no, it's nothing. How long do you think it will take you to get home?'

As we waited for Gemma, I bumbled about trying to change Lilly's nappy as DC Pawson carried on talking to me. To be honest, it was like white noise; I was too shocked to concentrate on what he was saying. Meanwhile, I could sense his colleague's eyes burning into me, watching my every move. It turned out that Gemma had previously shown the photographs to another girl at school. She had then told her parents about what she had seen, and they in turn had contacted the police.

Unbeknown to me, Lee was upstairs in his bedroom and had heard us talking. He rang Gemma and told her that two people were at the house asking questions about her. At this point, I was later to find out, Gemma worked out what was going on and proceeded to delete the incriminating photographs from her phone. She also went to see Mr Forrest to warn him that people were at her house, waiting to speak to her.

When Gemma eventually arrived home, she looked quite frightened and wanted to know what was going on. DC Pawson was very nice to her and calmly explained that they needed to speak to her about some pictures that she may have on her phone.

With that, Gemma shoved the phone at him. 'See for yourself,' she said. 'There's nothing on it. I don't know what you are talking about.'

But DC Pawson pressed Gemma a bit more. He explained to her that the police would be able to retrieve any photographs she may have deleted and that this was her opportunity to put the record straight.

It soon became plain that Gemma wasn't going to say anything more and shortly afterwards they left. DC Pawson said he would be back in touch on the Friday once he'd had a chance to investigate the phone.

At the time I believed Gemma was telling the truth. When they had gone, I turned to her, saying: 'Is there anything I should know? I do trust you, you know ...'

'Good,' she replied. 'You should.'

With that we ended the conversation and carried on as if nothing had happened.

Not surprisingly, I found it hard to sleep that night. My mind was all over the place and Lilly was unsettled. Paul and I talked and eventually we both fell asleep on the sofa and at around 3am I woke up when I heard Gemma coming down the stairs, dressed in her school uniform. Half awake, half asleep, I asked her what she was doing. 'It's the middle of the night, sweetheart, go back to bed,' I told her. And as if she was sleepwalking, back upstairs she went.

In the early hours, just as the alarm clock went off, I felt Gemma snuggling up to me. It was like she was a little girl again when she had climbed into my bed when she was ill or needed to be comforted. 'I just wanted a cuddle,' she explained. It was sweet, and yet I also remember thinking how out of character it was, even though we had an affectionate relationship. Of course, it all makes sense now ...

Later that day, Gemma called me from Ben's phone – hers had been confiscated – and asked if she could stay at Louise's that night. I told her that I didn't really like her staying over on a school night, but I thought it might be a good idea after what we had been through the night before. I felt she needed to be with her best friend, even if it was a school night – just this once.

Gemma came over to pick up her stuff and made a big fuss over Lilly. She then hugged me really tightly, and held my face in her hands and told me she loved me. When I told her I loved her, too, she grabbed me, this time holding my face more forcefully. 'No, Mum, you need to listen to me. I REALLY love you.' 'Yes, yes,' I said, 'I know you do. Now get out of here and try not to burn Louise's house down!'

I gave her some dinner money for tomorrow and off she went.

The next day she was gone.

CHAPTER 5

'WE KNOW WHO SHE'S WITH ...'

On Friday, 21 September 2012, less than 24 hours since I had packed Gemma off to Louise's for a sleepover, my whole world was turned upside down. And to think, I had started the day with nothing more to worry about than what kind of furniture we wanted to buy from Argos ...

Detective Constable Pawson and the school police officer came into the sitting room, where the family had gathered waiting for news. Our minds had been racing, trying to make sense of things and wondering what had happened to Gemma. No one wanted to admit their fears.

When DC Pawson then said, 'We know who she's with', I was chilled to the core.

The school police officer recapped the information that they had. Following DC Pawson's visit to us earlier in the week, he had been liaising with the school. The moment Gemma went missing, he requested that a number of cross-checks be made on Forrest.

DC Pawson's suspicions about Forrest had proved to be correct: he and Gemma were together.

'We have CCTV footage of Jeremy Forrest and Gemma boarding a ferry at 9.20pm last night from Dover to Calais. We tracked his car number plate from Eastbourne to the ferry crossing.'

I jumped up, screamed 'Nooooo,' and ran out of the room. Once again I found myself thinking, 'If I'm not there, it's not happening.' It can't be happening. I wanted to run, but I had nowhere to run to. My coping mechanism was to deny that my darling daughter could have been taken by this man. Things like this didn't happen to people like us.

Back in the sitting room with Paul, Max, Mum and Charlotte there was a whirlwind of questions. What was being done? When would they arrest him? When would Gemma be back? Did Gemma looked scared on the CCTV footage? Had he kidnapped her? Could he have molested her? Everyone wanted to speak; they wanted answers.

For me, it was just a blur. I went to the other side of the room trying to escape what I had just heard. Surely it is a mistake, I kept telling myself. Surely she will be home in a minute.

DC Pawson explained to us that Forrest had phoned in sick the day before. When the police report about Gemma going missing came through, he had called Forrest's home and spoken to his wife, who said he was away on a course in London. DC Pawson put two and two together – the rumours, the pictures, the pair of them going missing from school – and then it was just a matter of tracking down Forrest's car number plate.

By then, though, Forrest and Gemma had got a 15-hour head start on the police and were already over the border in France. The police said they were in contact with P&O Ferries and that officers were going to Dover to collect the CCTV images.

There was one glimmer of hope that we could all cling on to – Forrest had bought return tickets and they were due back in Dover on the 10pm ferry on Sunday night.

I tried to persuade myself that Gemma might ring me; after all, she would know how upset I would be that she had disappeared. I told myself maybe, just maybe, it was totally innocent, but deep down I knew I was kidding myself.

Paul was great and immediately took charge of the kids, making sure they were fed and tucked up in bed. Max was brilliant, too, doing everything he could. Everyone pulled together and tried to stay strong.

I didn't cry, and I didn't hassle the police to do more than they were doing already. I didn't feel any anger; in fact, I didn't feel any emotion at all – I was just numb. It was all too much for me to take in.

The sequence of events is a bit of a blur, but I do remember that at some stage a family liaison officer called Jim arrived. To start off with, he acted suspiciously with us, watching how we all interacted. I suppose he was trying to see if there was anything untoward going on. As we took calls from various family members and friends, he silently took it all in. It was a bit weird, but this was the least of my worries at the time.

I can't remember if I slept that night. From the moment I heard Gemma had gone missing, I stopped being myself. I felt like I was somehow on the outside, looking in, watching it all unfold. People were running around, fussing over me and the kids, trying to comfort me, encouraging me to eat and so on, but I was just blank. I started obsessing over stupid things. Would she have eaten? What clothes had she got with her? Does he know she is afraid of the dark?

But as I was soon to discover, the nightmare was only just beginning ...

CHAPTER 6

A WEEKEND
OF WAITING

On Saturday morning, Jim came back, and he was much more friendly this time than he had been the night before. In fact, over the course of the next few days we became like old friends. It is strange how quickly you bond with people in incredibly difficult circumstances.

The police issued us with a password, in case the press or anyone else got hold of the story and tried to get more information out of us over the phone. Bizarrely, our password was Wonga – apparently, it was the first thing Jim and his 'guvnor' had seen in the newspaper that morning. Soon after, I got a call from Detective Chief Inspector Jason Tingley but I refused to talk to him until I heard the magic password. I knew he was probably who he said he was, but I needed to make sure …

DCI Tingley, now armed with the right password, called us

back and later came over with a colleague, Detective Inspector Andy Harbour. They arrived at about 8pm and I sat in the kitchen with Paul, Max and my eldest sister Annette as the officers recounted what they knew. They explained that the CCTV images that P&O Ferries had provided were now with the police and a European arrest warrant was being prepared. Trouble was, it would need to be put before a senior judge in order for it to be authorised, and that couldn't happen until Monday morning at the earliest. That meant that if Gemma and Forrest didn't return on the Sunday night, they wouldn't be able to arrest him in France until Monday at the earliest.

They also explained to me how MI5 and the Serious Organised Crime Unit were advising Sussex Police, and how Interpol, the International Criminal Police Organisation, would assist with the investigation, acting as a go-between for the police forces in the UK and Europe. To be honest, I don't think I took it all in: all I wanted to know was how long it was going to take to bring my daughter back.

Annette and Max then started going on and on about the lack of support that the school had given us. It was then that I was broken out of my trance. I remember sitting there in utter disbelief at the conversation they were having.

Suddenly, I snapped. 'Will you two shut up! I don't care what your thoughts or views are, this is not helping. The only person I want to hear speak is Chief Inspector Tingley!' Having a debate about it wasn't going to get Gemma back.

At that point I didn't care what the school did or didn't do. I was just hanging on every word that Jason Tingley had to say. It wasn't until the next day, when it actually dawned on me what I had done, that I apologised for my outburst. I was ashamed about how I had reacted.

Jason explained that if Gemma and Forrest arrived back on the 10pm ferry, the police would be waiting there to arrest him on suspicion of abduction. They could do this as soon as they were back in the UK, but they couldn't do anything in France without the European arrest warrant. Once they had arrested Forrest, Gemma would then be taken into protective custody. She wouldn't be under arrest herself, as she had done nothing wrong.

Until then, he said, we just had to be patient ...

The next call I got was from the Sussex Police media department. With all the text messages and tweets that our family and friends had been putting out, our local newspaper, the *Eastbourne Herald*, had got hold of the story. To make matters worse, some other children at school had obviously put two and two together, and there were some Facebook messages going round, saying that Gemma had run off with Forrest.

The media department wanted to issue an official statement and take control of the situation. Max gave them a quote and, before we knew it, a story about Gemma appeared on the BBC News website ...

Missing schoolgirl XXXX XXXX thought to be in France
The parents of a 15-year-old East Sussex girl who is believed to have gone to France with a man she knows have urged her to contact them.
XXXX XXXX, from Eastbourne, was reported missing when she failed to turn up for school on Friday.
Sussex Police said she was spotted later using a Dover to Calais ferry.
Detectives named the man thought to be with XXXX as

Jeremy Forrest, 30, from Ringmer, near Lewes, who was driving a Ford Fiesta, registration GJ08 RJO.

The teenager's father, XXXX, said: 'We just want XXXX to make contact with us. We are worried and miss her terribly – please get in touch XXXX.'

Det Insp Andy Harbour from Sussex Police said: 'We do not believe XXXX to be at risk but we are appealing for her to make contact with her family, who are very worried and miss her.

'We know that she crossed from Dover to Calais at around 21:20 BST [on Friday]. We believe she is still in France and we are in contact with the French authorities.'

He urged anyone with information about her disappearance to contact the police.

XXXX is said to be 5ft 6ins, slim and has long dark brown hair. She was last seen wearing a white vest top and a silver necklace.

Once the story was out there, it spread like wildfire. I was quite naïve when it came to social media; I had only ever used Facebook for sharing pictures with my friends and family and had never used Twitter before. Max was much more techie, however, and by Sunday morning social media was going crazy with the story. Paul worked out how to set up a Twitter account and Lee and Maddie kept us up to date with everything they saw on Facebook.

Someone put up a post saying that Gemma had been abducted and I remember feeling sick to my stomach. That word had never been used before and seeing it written down made the situation even more frightening.

At some point I remember Lee telling us he had found a song that Forrest had posted on his blog under the name Jeremy Ayre and that people on social media were saying he had written it for Gemma. Lee wanted us to listen to it, but I couldn't face it. I just hoped that the press wouldn't pick up on it and make a story out of it.

Max had been looking after Alfie, but Monday was going to be his first day at school, so he brought him back to the house in the afternoon. I was determined that Alfie wasn't going to know what was happening. We told him that his big sister had gone to stay at her nan's, which wasn't unusual, as she often did.

Once I had tucked Alfie up in bed and settled Lilly, it was strange and eerily quiet in the house. Paul, Jim and I sat in the kitchen, drinking tea and watching the clock. Every so often, I would catch someone glancing up at the clock: we were all waiting for 10pm to come around.

It was the longest evening ever, but there really was nothing to do but wait. And wait. The clock was moving more slowly than ever. At one point, I even thought it was going backwards. It was unbearable.

Jim tried his best to keep our spirits up, reassuring us that the police would notify us the minute that the passenger lists had been checked on the ferry.

Ten pm came. No call. 10.05pm. No call. Then at 10.15pm, the phone rang. Jim walked into the hall and pulled the door behind him as Paul and I held each other and waited for him to come back in with good news.

A few minutes later, he walked back in, shaking his head: they weren't on the ferry. They were missing. At that point I allowed myself to cry. I completely broke down and fell into

Paul's arms, sobbing. My heart had literally been broken and every shred of emotion that I'd been holding back started flooding out.

I began blaming myself for everything that had happened. If only I'd listened to Gemma more ... If only I hadn't screamed and shouted at her because of that phone call from Forrest ... If only I hadn't said she could stay at Louise's ... It was all my fault. I have lived with that guilt ever since and I've had counselling to try and come to terms with it, but no amount of sessions will ever shed the guilt.

I was inconsolable. Paul and Jim tried to comfort me and insisted that I was not to blame in any shape or form, but it was all too much. I felt physically sick and sobbed my heart out. Then anger took over. I was filled with fury for that bastard. How dare Forrest do this to her? How could he ruin her life like this? What right did he have to take my daughter, to even be near her?

It was around this time that we discovered that the national papers were also interested in the story and had been trying to get more information out of Sussex Police. I was later to discover that the newspapers scour local websites for any stories that they can pick up on. In this case, *The Sun* was the first on the case.

We knew that the story was likely to be all over the papers the following day. My friend Chloe was due back from holiday in the early hours, so we sent her a text message asking her to pick up the first editions of all the newspapers at the airport when she arrived. My heart sank when she called me a few hours later: 'You're in all of the papers!' I insisted she read out every single story that had been written about Gemma. She said it was bizarre standing in the middle of Gatwick, reading out stories about a person she knew, but then nothing about this situation was exactly normal.

Each of the papers had put their own spin on the story, but basically they repeated what had been on the BBC News website. Luckily, the police hadn't revealed that Forrest was a teacher at Gemma's school, so that crucial piece of information was missing from those early stories.

By the time the later editions came out, though, they had unearthed more details. Suddenly we were faced with headlines such as MARRIED TEACHER ON RUN WITH PUPIL and YOU HIT ME LIKE HEROIN, which we later discovered was a line from the song that Forrest had apparently written for Gemma. There were pictures of Gemma in her school uniform, pictures of Forrest and his wife on their wedding day, pictures of the school ...

My private life had suddenly become very public.

CHAPTER 7

FAMILY TREE

When Gemma was born, on 2 June 1997, I made a promise to her that I would always love her and would never let anything bad happen to her. I had separated from her biological father Gary while I was pregnant. I was twenty-two; Gary was twenty-five. I remember telling her that day that it wouldn't matter that she didn't have two parents because I would always protect and love her more than two people put together.

Gary was my first love and our relationship was good to begin with. Shortly after we moved in together, I became pregnant with Lee and then three years later I discovered I was expecting again. At the time, Gary had a terrible temper and really scared me, so when I found out I was pregnant again, I decided to go it alone and bring up the children myself.

I tried again and again to get Gary to have some kind of

relationship with Lee and Gemma; I didn't want them not to have a father in their lives. But it was to no avail – he didn't even so much as hold Gemma until she was two weeks old and after that he only saw her a couple of times. He just didn't want to know her and Lee.

After that relationship, it wasn't a priority to meet anyone else, but two years later I met Max, and it was love at first sight. He was amazing with the children and we got married in Gretna Green on 23 October 1999. The children took his name and we were all really happy together. I gave birth to Maddie in 2000 and then, eight years later, Alfie came along.

Unfortunately, our relationship went downhill after Max was involved in a serious bike accident. He sustained terrible injuries to his back and had a year's rehabilitation. He kept reliving the nightmare of the accident and it was just too much strain on our marriage. We were unable to get it back on track and we agreed to separate when Alfie was two years old, but promised to stay as amicable as possible for the children's sakes. In fact we even spent a Christmas together as Max was determined to be a proper dad to the children. Later, Maddie moved in with him – she has always been Daddy's girl – but we are still very close and she comes and stays with us all the time, so I don't feel detached from her.

In 2010, I got promoted in my work as an auditor and it was there that I met Paul, who was a senior auditor. With four children already, I really had my hands full, but after much discussion we decided to try for a baby and were blessed with beautiful Lilly. Of course, the day she was born was the day that Miss Shackleton had called from Gemma's school about the rumours. For me, the first few months of Lilly's life were fairly dramatic, but through it all I was determined that Alfie and Lilly wouldn't be dragged into the nightmare.

I am extremely proud of the fact that we united as a family to keep Alfie and Lilly's lives as normal as possible. But things were about to get much more challenging ...

CHAPTER 8

NATIONAL AND INTERNATIONAL NEWS

During the course of Sunday night and into Monday morning I could hear the rumble of vehicles starting to descend on the street. By the morning the road was full of cars and vans set up with satellite dishes. There were swarms of photographers with tripods and zoom lenses aimed at our house.

My first priority was to get Alfie off for his first day of school. He didn't have a clue what was going on as we bustled around, getting his lunch box ready. He had his little book bag and a brand new school coat, and was really excited. I felt tearful because it was the first time that I hadn't been able to accompany one of my children on their first day at school, but Paul and I agreed that I should stay at home in case Gemma called. She didn't have her mobile phone with her, but we knew that she would remember the landline number.

There was an added complication: the phone account that we had at the house was in Max's name and we were in the process of changing it to my name and getting a new number. This wouldn't have mattered under normal circumstances, but it was meant to be changing that very day. I got in contact with the phone company, explained the situation and begged them not to change the number. Normally, it would have been too late, but luckily they were able to get engineers on the case and let us keep our original number.

My two best friends, Chloe and Darcee, arrived at around 8am and couldn't believe the crowd of reporters and TV crews that had gathered outside our house. They were shocked and frightened by the fact the story had escalated so quickly.

We kept all the curtains drawn and the blinds closed so that nobody could see in. I crawled around upstairs on my hands and knees, and started sitting on the floor instead of the bed in case the people who had gathered outside could see anything through a gap in the curtains. I know it's ridiculous, but I was becoming so paranoid that I started whispering to people, convinced the media gathered outside could somehow hear through the walls.

We could see that reporters were going round all of our neighbours, trying to dig up information, and we had a stream of people shoving business cards and scribbled notes through our letterbox, asking to speak to us. Anyone who came to the door got a very direct 'No comment' from Paul. He was the designated 'door opener' and the press soon got used to his response of 'No comment' every time.

At around 9am the post was delivered and there was a letter from Gemma's school. It said that she had to attend extra compulsory tuition lessons in maths. I couldn't believe what I was reading – not least because the maths teacher was Mr Forrest, the very same man who had just abducted my daughter and taken her to France! It was so shocking, it was almost laughable. What I said is unprintable, but you can probably guess the kind of thing ...

Chloe got straight on the phone to Mr Worship, the executive head of Kennedy High School; I was in too much of a rage to speak to him myself. There was an awkward silence, after which he apologised profusely and said that there must have been an oversight. The letter had been sent out on the Friday night and should have been intercepted, he explained, but it had slipped through the net.

It felt like such a smack in the face. Not only had the school had the cheek to get in touch about something so trivial at a time like this, it was about her abductor's specialist subject! I needed a lot of strong coffee to calm me down after that.

Next, a lady called Hannah called me and introduced herself as my new family liaison officer. It transpired that Jim had just been on duty over the weekend, although he was to help us again. Hannah explained that the Sussex Police media team wanted to set up a press conference with me and Max. She told me a bit about what would be involved and instructed me to be ready to be picked up at midday.

I was terrified. I hate being in the spotlight – I didn't even like walking down the aisle at my own wedding – and the idea of everyone looking at me and having cameras in my face scared the hell out of me. The fact that it was because my darling daughter had gone missing only made it worse: it was almost too much to bear.

Hannah informed me that the press conference would be

covered by all the major national networks, including the BBC, ITN and Sky, and that there would also be a French translator present so that the story could be broadcast in France, too.

As much as the idea of the press conference filled me with horror, I knew how important it was to get the message out about Gemma. No matter what, I had to go through with it. I had been living in baggy pregnancy clothes since Lilly was born and hadn't give a second thought to what kind of state my hair or clothes were in. My image was the least of my worries, but Chloe and Darcee were brilliant and helped me to look as presentable as I could under the circumstances.

At midday, Hannah arrived. Chloe, Darcee and I stepped out of the house with our heads ducked down and headed for the waiting unmarked police car. We had agreed that Paul would stay at home to man the phones in case Gemma saw the press conference and got in touch.

At this point, the reporters didn't know what I looked like, so I hoped that having my friends with me might mean they wouldn't single me out. I couldn't believe the deafening noise when I walked out into the street. There was an immediate click-click-click-click-click as the photographers craned to get pictures and there were people shouting out questions from every direction. 'Can you tell us any more?' 'How are you feeling?' 'Are there any more details you can share with us?' 'Has she been in touch?'

It was so scary. Every time I tried to look up and see what was going on, everything went white as the flashbulbs blinded me.

During the 20-minute journey, Hannah tried to keep the conversation light, explaining who she was and how I could contact her at any time after the press conference had taken place. She was clearly trying to calm my nerves, but there was nothing anybody could say or do to stop me feeling scared.

When we arrived at Sussex Police HQ, there were more reporters and cameras waiting for us outside, so we went in through the back and walked through a maze of corridors to reach the conference area.

DCI Jason Tingley came in and explained what was going to happen that afternoon. I remember asking him if he had ever done anything like this before, and was relieved when he said he hadn't. It made me feel a bit less anxious to think that we were both going through it for the first time. He kept disappearing and I later discovered that, like me, he was petrified and had to keep visiting the bathroom whenever anyone mentioned the words 'TV cameras'.

Nick Cloke, the media team's head of communications strategy, introduced me to Neil Honour, the chief superintendent of Sussex Police. Normally, I would have been in awe of meeting someone of his standing, but it didn't feel significant at the time. It was more about finding out what each of these people were doing to help me find my daughter. I was reassured that so much was being done and I was incredibly grateful.

By this time Max had arrived and we were asked to each prepare a script to read out to the press. Nick explained that this was in case we went blank when it came to the time for each of us to speak.

How on earth could I convey how I felt? I thought about other police conferences where parents had put out pleas for lost children that I had seen on television. I knew how important it was to make the most of every second I was allowed to speak and to say something that would reach out to Gemma if she saw the message.

Before we knew it, it was time to go in and face the press. I remember looking at Max's face and he was as white as a sheet. We gave each other a reassuring smile and then went in.

Once again, there was that click-click-click-click-click of cameras going off all around us and a blinding of white flashbulbs. I started shaking like a leaf; I couldn't control myself. I took my seat and sat on my hands, desperate to stop the shaking. I knew how important this opportunity was. I told myself that it didn't matter how I was feeling, it was all about getting Gemma back. Nothing else mattered.

I was sitting at one end of a long table. Max was next to me, followed by Jason Tingley and then the French translator. Jason kicked off proceedings by reading out a press statement and explained the situation with the French authorities and what was happening with the European arrest warrant – basically, that everything was being put in place to get Gemma back as soon as possible.

Then it was time for me to read out my statement. As Nick Cloke had warned, my mind did go blank, so I was glad of my piece of paper with the words I wanted to say to Gemma.

This is what I said:

Sweetheart, I don't care what you have done or why. You can tell I'm in pieces and I just want you home. Your brother is absolutely devastated. Lee is beside himself and wants you back; Alfie keeps asking where you are; Maddie is walking around in a daze. She won't leave my side and keeps asking when are you going to come home. And from me to you, sweetheart, you know that your adorable princess wants her adorable mermaid back. So please, darling, do anything. Text me, ring me, send me a message on Facebook, just do anything. The phone number at home hasn't changed, so just ring me, please, sweetheart.

As I was saying the bit about adorable princess and adorable mermaid, I made a shape like angel wings above my head. It was something Gemma always did with Lilly; there is such a special bond between the two of them. It might have looked a bit silly, but I knew that if Gemma saw it, she would know I was reaching out to her.

Max spoke next, reiterating what I had said and saying we were a really close family and so wanted her back.

Once we had all had our turn to speak, there was a question-and-answer session with the press. The floodgates opened as all the reporters started shouting questions at me. After a while, Jason Tingley stepped in. He could see that it was all getting too much for me and he said that questions should be addressed to him only. He didn't reveal all the facts about the case as it was important to hold back various details. That way, if anybody came forward with any information, the police could verify that it tallied with their own information.

After about 20 minutes, the press conference was over and Max and I left the room. The moment I got through the door, I collapsed to the floor and started howling like a wounded animal. I don't remember any of this. It was like I'd passed out, unaware of my actions, but Chloe and Darcee said the noise I was making was almost inhuman, and they were very upset about the state I was in. They helped me to my feet and kept talking to bring me back round.

A little while later, once I'd had a chance to compose myself, Max and I did an interview with a journalist from ITV's

Daybreak, which was then circulated to other broadcasters. We only agreed to this because we knew how important it was to get the story out. If anyone thinks you get to feel like a celebrity when this sort of thing is going on, you are very much mistaken. The whole experience made me feel sick.

I was completely shell-shocked and felt utterly exhausted, but the police media team reassured us that what we had done would create the best possible press coverage for the search to find Gemma and Forrest. Nick Cloke said we had done really well.

Back in the car on the way home, Hannah asked me a question which no mother should ever have to hear: 'When Gemma is found, do you give your permission for her to be medically examined once she is taken into protective custody?' My heart went cold. To be fair to her, Hannah had to ask me that question and she quickly explained that if Gemma didn't agree to an examination, they wouldn't force her.

Even at this point, when I knew there was a sexual issue to consider, I just wanted to block it out. I wasn't being naïve about it, I just couldn't face the idea of my little girl and this wicked, predatory teacher together.

Luckily for me, there were other things to consider. Paul had picked up Alfie after his first day at school and taken him to McDonald's as a special treat, and I was determined to give him the fuss he deserved when I got home. I ran into the house, scooped him up in my arms and gave him the biggest cuddle ever. It was as if I had an on-off switch – seeing Alfie's happy little face helped me step out of the Gemma nightmare and switch back into normal life. To totally put aside problems and concentrate on getting the necessary done is a great coping mechanism.

Alfie was desperate to tell me all about his first day at school, what he had done, what his teachers were like and the new friends that he had made. He is such a lovely, friendly little boy and always so enthusiastic. He was really excited and almost bouncing off the walls, filling me in on his day. I made a special point of saying how grown-up he was, going off to big school now.

We knew that details from the press conference and Gemma's photograph were likely to be all over the television news reports, so Paul hid the remote control to make sure that Alfie wouldn't switch on and see his big sister on TV. Like every child, Alfie loves to watch the telly, so instead we said he could watch a movie before he went to bed as a treat. We told him that we had turned the house into a special cinema and that was why all the curtains were drawn and the blinds were down.

To this day, Alfie and Lilly have no idea about anything that has happened, and it is something I am extremely proud of.

As we were enjoying family time with Alfie, the phone rang. It was Mr Worship, from Gemma's school. This was the first contact that I'd had with the school for days, apart from a rather random call from someone called Mr Corbitt, who was clearly clueless about the situation. He wanted to know the details of the case and said, 'I'll be at the school until four pm. If you find her can you call me back?' Then he rang off without giving me his number.

While I was trying to remain calm for Alfie's sake, I took the call in the back garden and gave Mr Worship five barrels of my fury. I told him that I was absolutely disgusted with the school and the insulting lack of contact and support that I'd had. I told him my mother and sister had been over to the school on the Friday to see if they could find out any information and all they had been offered was a cup of tea and a prayer. And as for that letter about extra maths tuition … That was just a sick joke.

What Mr Worship then said to me wound me up even more. He told me that he had been at his desk all weekend and made a special point of telling me that he'd given up his weekend and his family time to be there – as if I should be grateful after all the hell that his school had put me through!

But I needed answers; I also needed practical advice about what to do. So far, all I'd got from the school was a head teacher who had generously given up his weekend to wait for news! I couldn't have been angrier.

After that, the phone never seemed to stop ringing. Next, I got a call and a visit from Mark Ling, the chief inspector for child protection, who wanted to conduct another search through Gemma's room to see if there was any evidence that they had missed previously.

Then Mum called to say a family friend had volunteered to create a website dedicated to finding Gemma. Over the course of the next few days, it proved to be incredibly useful. Unfortunately, though, other bogus 'Find Gemma' sites started cropping up, with pictures taken from her Facebook and Twitter accounts, and there were all sorts of sick people pretending to be her. With each day that passed, I became increasingly disturbed by the way that some people could behave.

Lee was particularly furious about the stuff that people were writing on social media sites and took it really badly. I kept trying to reassure him that it didn't matter what they were saying, that we knew the real Gemma and that everything was being done to get his sister back.

Finally, on Monday evening, when the police had finished searching Gemma's room again and my two youngest were in bed, we sat down to watch all of the news programmes that we had recorded on Sky+. It was punishing to see the same report over and over again, my darling daughter's face taking over the whole of the screen. We sat up until the early hours watching different channels' coverage of the same footage, hoping against hope that there would be some breaking news or the phone might ring and it would be Gemma, saying she was coming home.

CHAPTER 9

NO CONTACT, PLEASE

As Monday had been such a full-on and emotional day, with so many significant things happening, I decided to ban everyone from coming round on Tuesday – even my best friends: I wanted to concentrate on Paul and the kids. The two little ones were too small to know what was going on, but I could sense uneasiness. Paul was finding it a strain and Lee and Maddie were very unsettled about all the rubbish on social media.

We needed some time to regroup as a family. I felt ashamed about my outburst on Sunday when I lost my temper with Annette and Max – it just didn't feel like me – and I felt that I needed to get myself back on track and focus on staying positive.

I banned everyone from using the landline, so that it would be clear for Gemma if she were to ring, and I had my mobile phone practically super-glued to my side in case there was any news from the police.

My neighbours were all completely fantastic while the madness was going on outside my front door. They spoke to reporters, but nobody said anything derogatory or tried to stitch us up; everyone was so respectful. I felt so terrible that they were trapped in their homes while the press took over the street, but they were all very patient about it.

My next-door neighbour Katrina was an absolute star. As it was so difficult for us to leave the house, she started handing food parcels over the garden fence. She made sure we had enough food in for the kids and plenty of milk for all of those endless cups of tea and coffee that we were going through. I don't know how I would have managed without her.

Tuesday was spent trying to do ordinary family things, the things I felt that I had neglected for the past few days. Paul had taken over feeding and changing Lilly, so I made a special point of taking back the reins as far as being the mum was concerned. I needed to let my children know I was still there for them and give them as much reassurance as I could that everything would be alright. I also needed the time to find the energy for whatever was to happen next.

Hannah called me with the great news that the European arrest warrant had been issued and let me know that there had been a fantastic response to the press conference. The police were busy sifting through leads, Detective Inspector Andy Harbour was on his way to the incident room that had been set up in Paris, and officers were on standby to collect Gemma and bring her back to the UK when she was found.

I sent Andy Harbour a text message to wish him good luck and thanked him for everything he was doing. His reply read: 'I promise I will do everything to bring her back'. It brought tears to my eyes. I was overwhelmed by the care we were getting. My world was in his hands and I knew I could completely trust him.

Later that day, Hannah came over with the CCTV images that were going to be released to the media. They showed Gemma hand in hand with Forrest. She was wearing her school uniform but had swapped her school polo top for a vest top. 'At least she looks OK,' I remember thinking. 'She doesn't look frightened, she looks quite relaxed – oh, and she's wearing my cardigan!' I felt so relieved to see a picture of her, but the sight of her hand in hand with her teacher was another thing altogether. I didn't want to think about it too much, I couldn't go there.

I kept staring at the picture. All the while I kept thinking, how could I have missed this? I remembered conversations, days when she had gone out, and I wondered if there had been any times she had given me hints that something else was going on.

In contrast to the day before, Tuesday was quite a calm day for all of us. Alfie went off to school as normal, but I could see that he was a bit confused about all the people outside and the fact we were still living in the dark inside the house.

One time, when Alfie asked why there were so many people outside, Max told him that the next-door neighbours were having a party. Alfie believed him, but he was very disappointed that he hadn't been invited! On the two occasions when he saw police officers in the house, they were in plain clothes, so Paul and I told him they were from Argos and had come round to find out if he had been good enough for the Spiderman helicopter that he wanted. It's amazing how creative you can become in a crisis.

Later that day, an intelligence officer came over to fit a tracking device to our phone and we told Alfie he was mending it. The whole thing was such a strange situation – like I was in an episode of *24* or something. I just couldn't take the information in. The poor officer kept demonstrating what to do, if and when Gemma was to call, but I was all fingers and thumbs.

Hannah called again and asked me to check which clothes Gemma might have taken so that they could be matched up with the sightings that were coming through. She explained that the officers had taken what they thought was significant – scribbles on paper, her diary, her old mobile phone – but she said I might also be able to find things that the police had overlooked.

I was completely freaked out at the prospect of going back into her bedroom. When I'd been in the room on Friday, it was before the nightmare had really started, and I hadn't been back in there since. At that point, I thought she was just absent from school, not officially missing. Now, of course, things were much more serious. I remember standing outside her bedroom door and being frozen to the spot. I told myself I had to do this and I put my hand on the door lever, pushing it down as if it was a 10-ton weight. My subconscious had taken over and I'd lost all strength in my body. Once again, it was like being on the outside, watching myself going through the motions.

When I eventually got in the room, I was shocked back to life when I discovered that the police had tidied up. Almost unrecognisable, in a way, it didn't feel like her room at all. It helped, though, because it switched me back to reality and the task in hand.

Gemma had a big plastic storage tub under her bed and I went through it. There were the things I expected, like magazines and posters and the various autographs she had collected but I also came across a ripped-up 'Boyfriend' birthday card and some CDs that didn't seem to be hers; they weren't the kind of bands she would usually like. I also found some verses written down which looked like song lyrics. There was one sheet with two people's handwriting on it – hers and someone else's. They had obviously written a song together. I could only guess who the other writing belonged to ...

Although I had tried to use the day to just be with Paul and the children, Mum was so distraught about what was going on that I was happy for her to come over that evening with my sister Charlotte. Mum and Gemma had always been close and she really wasn't coping well. I tried to reassure her that the police were doing everything in their power to get Gemma back. In a way, I gave her the kind of debriefing that the police had been giving me.

Once they had left, and Alfie and Lilly were in bed, Paul and I lay on the sofa together with our laptop and tried to make sense of it all. Social media was going crazy and there seemed to be all sorts of information out there that I had no idea about. Gemma not only posted on Facebook and Twitter, but she also had Tumblr and Instagram accounts, and it was like a feeding frenzy on social media. The press, internet trolls and just about anyone we could think of seemed to have raked through Gemma's files and reproduced her pictures. The comments on the various posts that were appearing were horrific – and extremely personal.

I felt terrible that I hadn't done more to protect her privacy. I'd always believed that I had been a good mum in that way –

whenever there was anything on TV about eating disorders, internet grooming and any other issues that particularly affected teenagers, I practically forced my children to watch them so that they would be savvy about what they revealed online.

There was once a documentary on television about a man who had pretended to be a young girl online in order to meet other young girls. I wanted my children to understand that unless you physically know the person you are in touch with on social media, then they are not your friend. I used to make them all tell me who each of their friends on Facebook were and explain to me how they knew that person, and I gave them a limit for how much time they could spend on the computer each day. I also put firewalls and parental controls on devices, but obviously this hadn't been enough.

On occasion, I had even done random searches through their phones for pictures and messages, but clearly I hadn't been as vigilant as I had needed to be. I blamed myself and couldn't believe how naïve I'd been to think I could control what was out there.

I now know that social media is virtually impossible to control. It was like wildfire. I couldn't believe how many friend requests I had on Facebook. People I hadn't heard from for years were coming out of the woodwork to re-connect with me, not to mention all the strangers who wanted to know me all of a sudden.

I have always been very wary of strangers around my children. When I first got together with Max, and then later with Paul, I was very mindful about how they interacted with my children. Changing nappies and bathing has always been my domain, and when it came to cuddling I watched them like a hawk until I was completely convinced I could trust them. I know I'm probably overly cautious, but I have subsequently discussed it with them both and they said they wouldn't expect me to behave any differently anyway.

It was at this point, when all these outsiders suddenly wanted to be friends, that I had a real crisis of trust. It seemed my family was fair game for anyone to comment on, write about and exploit.

Someone had seen a bucket list that Gemma had created on Tumblr, another social media site that I previously knew nothing about. The list included all the things that you would expect a teenager to want to do – learn to drive, go to Glastonbury, visit Niagara Falls, go in a hot air balloon, etc. – but there were also other items that she had already crossed out. She had fulfilled her 'Go to Hollywood' dream during the half-term school trip to America, where she was seen holding hands with Forrest, but there were other items she had crossed out that the press were to pick up on: 'Number 7: Have someone write a song about me' and 'Number 50: Fall in love'. Before Gemma had disappeared I'd never known her to be in love before.

What was crazy was that all of this information was just out there online, and we hadn't needed to do much digging around to find it. Throughout the whole process, I used to get Paul to buy all of the papers, but I hadn't been able to face reading them. All of the new information I was getting was online.

Then there was yet another revelation to prepare for – the press had found out that Max wasn't Gemma's biological father. Although I told my family about not talking to the press, my sister Macy had been interviewed by a reporter and, because she wasn't used to the way the press were able to wheedle information out, had inadvertently spilled the beans on a few things. When the reporter asked, 'Gemma's real dad is Max, isn't he?' She said 'Oh no, that's not Max, his name is Gary Walker.' Yet more headline fodder.

I felt upset and betrayed, and it all added to the feeling I had that I couldn't trust anyone. The fact that people seemed to be finding out things before I knew about them made me feel even less of a parent than I already did.

CHAPTER 10

'TELL ME
THE TRUTH'

Paul and I didn't go to bed that night. We just stayed on the sofa, looking at social media, hardly believing the depths that some people could sink to. There was even a website of jokes dedicated to Gemma and Forrest. How could people be so sick?

I knew we shouldn't keep reading, but it was like a drug. I had given birth to Gemma, my beautiful mermaid, but all these people were trying to own a piece of her, like tragedy vampires.

I remember standing in the shower at 3am on Wednesday morning in a total daze. Convinced she was dead, I cried and cried and cried. It was so black outside and so bleak inside the house, everything seemed to be against us. I was in the depths of my despair, I honestly didn't think I could ever feel worse; there was nowhere further to fall.

Chloe came round early on Wednesday morning and asked me what kind of night I'd had. I told her that I had a terrible feeling that Gemma was dead and she insisted straight away that I ask the police directly, in case it turned out that they were withholding information from me for some reason. If she was dead, then maybe they weren't saying anything so they had more chance of catching Forrest. And if he was a murderer, he would definitely be on the run.

I'd been looking at a picture of Forrest and trying to 'read' his face and find out what kind of person he was. To me, he was nothing to look at, not handsome in the slightest – if anything, I thought he was a bit strange-looking. But at that moment in time, I hoped and prayed that deep down he loved Gemma. That way, he would never physically harm her.

I still wouldn't allow myself to think about the two of them sexually. He was her teacher, she was a schoolgirl and half his age. It was almost as if by blocking out these thoughts I could stop them from happening. Obviously this wasn't the case – I couldn't prevent something happening by just avoiding it – but at the time I had to do whatever worked for me. I was in denial, but the alternative was just too much to bear.

I'd been shocked to find the torn-up 'Boyfriend' birthday card among Gemma's things. When I told Charlotte about it, her face dropped. 'Oh my God! During the summer, Gemma mentioned she had a boyfriend called Jeremy ...' She had forgotten his name at the time and later, when she asked Gemma again if she had a boyfriend, she'd just laughed it off, saying, 'No, I'm not interested. Mum has put me off!'

Some people have asked me if I was ever tempted to contact Forrest's parents or his wife, but I just didn't want to be involved with them. One of the police officers told me that his parents had sent a message to say they were thinking of me and would do anything to help. Although genuinely touched by their concern, I didn't feel it would help the situation to contact them.

Later that morning Chief Inspector Mark Ling and his colleague, Detective Inspector Neil Ralph, came to the house to update me on how things were progressing. As soon as they walked through the door, Chloe made me ask them if Gemma was dead. I didn't want to hear the answer, but I had to know whether, in their hearts, their investigations to find her were in vain.

Without any hesitation, Mark Ling said that he truly believed Gemma was still alive and went on to tell me about a number of unconfirmed sightings that had been reported. There was nothing concrete at that stage, but officers were working round the clock.

He also explained how a detailed chain of command had been set up. There were three stages – bronze, silver and gold – to process evidence as it came through. Our conversation made me feel a lot more confident that the police were doing absolutely everything they possibly could do to find Gemma.

At some stage one of the newspapers put out a stupid story claiming that the French authorities weren't cooperating with the investigation. That couldn't have been further from the truth: the police had been in touch with the police forces in France, Belgium, Germany, Holland, Italy, Spain and even further afield, so there was a whole network of support for us. We were so angry that this spurious story could jeopardise the investigations and the goodwill that had been developing. The paper was ordered to print an apology and luckily no damage was done.

Following our press conference, Mark Ling told us that Forrest's parents had agreed to do their own press appeal on Thursday, as it might help the investigation. Apparently, Forrest's father had said that he was concerned about his son's state of mind, but that statement had been retracted. Mark Ling felt the need to tell me this as he didn't want me to subsequently hear about it and worry.

I was later to discover that Forrest allegedly had mental health issues. Even now I can't bear to think about what they could have been, or what the implications might have been for Gemma if the pressure had all become too much for him while they were in France. What if he had lost his mind and hurt her?

As well as being in touch with Forrest's parents, the police had spoken to his wife Emily about the situation before he disappeared. She had told them that they had been having some marital difficulties, but that they had been out to dinner on the previous Wednesday night and had agreed to work through their problems. When he disappeared, she said it had hit her like a brick wall.

The police had traced Forrest's bank details and could see that he had taken out a large sum of cash before he and Gemma left the country. They didn't tell me exactly how much, but they had worked out how long it would last if they were frugal and eked the money out. The police were hoping Forrest would eventually use one of his bank cards because then it would instantly be traced, but he would most likely have known this, hence him taking out a wad of cash before they fled.

Everyone seemed to be offering the police as much help as they could. The only person who was hindering the investigation was Gemma's friend Louise. She had been questioned on a number of occasions, but had given different accounts about what had happened.

I felt a little sorry for Louise. Obviously caught between a rock and a hard place, she was trying to stand by her best friend and was scared to be facing the police. Meanwhile, her stories were getting more and more convoluted. I was told that further measures might have to be taken if she continued to refuse to cooperate with the police, as she was holding up the investigation, and I promised that I would contact her the next day.

At the end of Mark Ling's visit, I truly felt that everything that could be done was being done. Even so, I wanted to be in France, looking for Gemma myself. I turned around to Chloe and said: 'I need to do something, I need to go out there and look for her. I can't keep sitting here feeling like I'm doing nothing.'

Without missing a beat, she said: 'Fine, there's nothing stopping you. We can get on the Eurostar and be in France in a couple of hours. Then what are you going to do? Do you know how big France is? What if they aren't even in France now? What happens if she calls? What then?'

I felt useless at home just waiting, but Chloe stopped me in my tracks and made me think again. 'Everything that can be done is being done,' she said. 'You have everyone working twenty-four hours, looking for her. You need to be here for when she calls. You're providing the police with every single piece of information you know. What more can you do? Think about it seriously for a moment. What your family really needs is to have you here. You need to be here for when Gemma comes back.'

And I realised that Chloe was right. I knew I needed to stay at home, but I wanted to be sure I hadn't missed anything with so much going on. I knew the police might call, asking for more information or for me to go somewhere at any point, and I couldn't do that if I was in France. More importantly, Gemma might phone and there was no way I would want to miss that.

That evening, Max called me and told me that he had also been thinking about going to France. A TV company had been in touch with him and wanted to take a film crew to France and start their own investigation. I could understand why he wanted to get involved, but I told him that he shouldn't, as there was more going on than I could tell him about at the moment.

At that stage I couldn't tell him about the unconfirmed sightings, or the chain of command that had been put in place and the fact that Forrest's bank account was being monitored. The police didn't want full disclosure of how Gemma and Forrest were being tracked down. They had told me because I was the parent with responsibility, but I had to keep that information to myself. I promised Max that I would tell him as soon as I possibly could. He was disappointed, but he understood that I had my reasons.

By 10pm, the phone calls seemed to stop for the night. The reporters outside had gone home and Paul and I were able to sit together and talk through the day's events once again.

That night, the television presenter Anne Diamond appeared on *Sky News* as part of a panel of guests previewing the following day's newspapers. I couldn't believe it when she described the story as 'a bit so-whatish'. The fact that Gemma was fifteen and Forrest was 'twenty-something' – even though he was actually thirty – wasn't, she said, a 'sickeningly huge age gap'.

I couldn't believe what I was hearing. She said that he must be tracked down and brought to book for the offence, but she was talking about it as if it wasn't a big deal. She seemed unable to see that she was actually talking about child abuse. We were absolutely seething.

One thing that did lighten the day was that the daughter of one of our neighbours, who we barely knew, had been interviewed in the *Daily Mail*. In the piece, she claimed to be a 'close friend' of Gemma's, although as far as we knew they had never hung out together or socialised at all. However, she very kindly said that it was completely unlike Gemma to run away and we were all in shock, and that we were a very nice family – which was nice! It was just another example of the crazy 'extra' things that we had to deal with while this whole situation was going on.

We then watched TV into the night to see what news had come out that day. I dreaded turning it off, for it all to go eerily quiet. For me, when the noise stopped, the searching stopped. I didn't think about the fact that it was a 24-hour operation for the police. I lived for the morning to arrive when everything felt like it started up again, when I knew that people were still searching, still getting the message out that my daughter was missing.

CHAPTER 11

THE WAITING GAME CONTINUES

Sure enough, around 7am the following morning, the newspaper reporters and television cameras returned and took up their pitches outside the house. It seemed strange how quickly we had fallen into a pattern of living – another day camped out on the street for the press pack, another day of waiting in the kitchen of our blacked-out house for us.

As usual, the post arrived early. To add to all of the madness in the street, we started receiving letters from complete strangers. They would have the words 'To the parents of Gemma Grant, Eastbourne' on the front of them and yet, unbelievably, they still somehow got to us, like those letters addressed to 'Father Christmas, Lapland' you hear about.

I received some saying 'God will protect your daughter, God will keep her safe'. I'm not a religious person, but I didn't mind well-wishers saying things like that. It was comforting to know that Gemma's story had touched them enough for them to take the time to write to us.

But not all the letters were positive. Some, frankly, were just plain disturbing. One in particular I remember was from a retired schoolteacher, who wrote: 'You need to let your daughter be with this man. She loves him and you should let the relationship continue.' He said it wasn't important what I believed and that Gemma was entitled to do what she wanted.

I couldn't believe how some people felt they were entitled to wade in with opinions on good parenting. I received letters, some from other parents of teenage children who should know better, saying, 'She's nearly sixteen, she's free to do what she wants'. To read stuff like this was so upsetting. How could these people not understand that this was abuse, not romance? Gemma had only turned fifteen in June, so presumably the 'relationship' had started when she was still fourteen.

Gemma was my little girl; Jeremy Forrest was a predatory monster.

Being a small neighbourhood, I knew the postman, and he would look a bit sheepish when he knocked on the door with armfuls of mail. He was very respectful, though, and even months later would ask us if we were OK and tell us if reporters were still hanging around. It was incredible, the amount of support we got from the most unlikely people.

Darcee arrived quite early and helped me get through all the 'normal' things – getting Lilly settled, getting Alfie off to school, and so on – and tried to make me eat something. I'd been surviving on coffee for the past few days; I just wasn't interested in food. Over the course of that week, I lost a stone, but I can assure you that it is not a diet I would recommend.

One of the first phone calls I received that day was from

the Sussex Police media team, telling me that the BBC1 programme *Crimewatch* was planning to run a report on Gemma that night and asking me if I would be prepared to appear on it. As before, my immediate reaction was: 'Will it help bring back my daughter?' The police media team were very honest with me. They said it wouldn't necessarily make a difference, and there was already much going on in France which the press didn't know about, but equally it wouldn't do any harm either. I didn't like the idea of leaving the house for the day – Gemma could call at any time, after all, and I had the other children to consider – so it was agreed that Max would do it instead.

Darcee and I spent the remainder of the day waiting for news. At that stage, I felt as if everything was out of my control and that I had pretty much done all that I could. I logged on to Facebook and tried to catch up with everything that was happening on social media. There were lots of messages from well-wishers and an old school friend of Gemma's had set up a Facebook support group. She became my eyes and ears as to what was happening on social media and was good at warning me if someone was being more interested in the case than they should be – she could spot disturbed people very quickly!

The press, meanwhile, had found more songs online that Forrest had written for Gemma. They also started to piece together Twitter conversations that Gemma and Forrest had shared and random comments that she had posted on Facebook. If there was anything to be dug up, it seemed the newspapers managed to find it.

At 3pm that day, Forrest's parents, Jim and Julie, appeared at a press conference at Lewes police station. I only got to see it much later in the day and, to be honest, I wasn't all that interested in what they had to say; I was more interested in what they looked like and whether they seemed like good people. I could instantly see the pain on their faces. I could see his mother's fear, the worry, the strain and devastation. I could hear his father's voice shaking as he tried to hold it together. I walked away from the TV with a very saddened heart. What a mess ...

Following Mark Ling's conversations the day before, his colleague, Neil Ralph, called to ask if I would send Louise a text to see if I could get her to open up to me about Gemma. I realised it was a very scary thing for her to be going through, but at this stage it was crucial that she told me the truth.

This is what I wrote to Louise:

Hi honey, it's Gem's mum. Sweetheart, first of all I just wanted to check you're OK? It's been horrible not to have seen you since this started as I'm guessing you're so upset. It's been like living out a nightmare here. Lee keeps crying, Maddie is beside herself and Alfie keeps asking where she is. As for Lilly, we say a little prayer every night for her 'adorable mermaid' to come home. Paul and I are a mess and keep asking ourselves why we didn't spot the fact she would leave us. As for me, I can't sleep, can't eat and I'm so so worried that she's dead. I can't stop crying and I haven't left the house in case she calls me. I've managed to keep the home number the same as I know she'll know it. I had to do that press conference and it was the worst thing I've ever done. I got outside and collapsed on the floor and sobbed my heart out. If she doesn't want to come home, that has to be her choice. I just need to know that she is safe, well and alive. Sending lots of love and hugs and you know where we are if you want to talk.

Her reply didn't contain any useful information. All she said was: 'Hi, I'm okay, just praying for Gem's safe return. Thinking of you all. Love Louise.'

I later found out that the reply had been scripted by Louise's mother. I wasn't surprised, as I imagine she may have thought Louise was an 'accessory to the crime' or something like that. Although I understood why she replied that way, it was so frustrating.

Nothing really seemed to be moving forward. I wondered how much more of it I could take.

We watched *Crimewatch* later that evening and Max came over extremely well on the programme. I was really proud of him and I remember thinking what a shame it was that he was referred to as Gemma's stepfather. Max had always been a wonderful father to Gemma and brought her up as if she was his own, and I felt really sorry for him in that respect. He'd been more of a father to her than her biological dad ever had.

The next day, Friday, 28 September, began in much the same way as the one before. Chloe came over and helped me with the morning routine as the media once again descended on the street and took up their positions outside our house.

As usual, Paul was at his sentry post at the front door, ready to face the barrage of reporters asking for more information. Chloe and I were talking in the kitchen when I realised he was having a much longer conversation than usual with one of the reporters. He came into the kitchen and told us that a journalist from the *Daily Mail* had come up with an idea that he thought we should consider – writing a letter to Gemma that they would publish in the newspaper.

Unlike the other requests we'd had, we thought this idea actually sounded constructive. First, though, I wanted to talk it through with Nick Cloke, the head of Sussex Police's media team – I wasn't going to do anything without the police's approval. When I called him, he seemed a bit lukewarm about the idea. He explained that he was on a train so he couldn't talk properly and would get back to me about it as soon as he could. He sounded a bit off with me and I wondered if I'd said something to annoy him.

I was a bit disappointed – I wanted to do something proactive instead of just sitting around, waiting for the phone to ring. Paul was confused and disappointed, too.

Little did we know but Nick Cloke had just received more information about Gemma …

A little while later, at 12.30pm, the phone rang.

It was Hannah. She sounded very serious as she confirmed it was really me that she was talking to, and my heart skipped a beat.

Then she said the words we had all been desperate to hear: 'We've got her!'

CHAPTER 12

SHE'S SAFE

I screamed and screamed with every breath in my lungs. Poor Paul didn't know what the hell was going on.

He wondered if it was terrible news and looked ashen as he ran in and found me holding my head as I tried to find out more information from Hannah. I turned to him and said: 'It's OK, they've got her!'

Chloe and Lee had popped out to get us fish and chips for lunch, and they came back to find Paul and me jumping around the kitchen with joy. There were chips flying everywhere as we all hugged each other and danced around – it was madness, the best feeling in the world. I didn't know what to do with myself. Excited, thrilled, relieved, hysterical ... I wanted to run out into the road, screaming 'They've got her, they've got her!'

Sky News had been on in the living room and almost immediately a ticker- tape news alert appeared on screen: GEMMA GRANT FOUND. Meanwhile, I was frantically phoning Mum and Max, and trying to Facebook friends and text people to say she was safe.

I couldn't believe how quickly the news filtered through on social media; it was mayhem in the house with all the phone calls. Chloe tried to encourage me to get dressed and ready for when Hannah came to pick me up, but I didn't want to leave the kitchen as that was where I had received the good news. I didn't want the bubble to burst. The adrenaline was just incredible.

At 1pm, Hannah arrived and warned me to be prepared for even more reporters than before. There were swarms of them outside the house and I wondered if we were going to be able to get out of the street. As soon as we opened the front door, the cameras and questions started firing. 'How do you feel about the news?' 'Are you flying out to see her?' 'Are there any comments you'd like to make?' It was crazy.

I remember thinking how frightening it must be to be famous and to have to deal with this kind of press attention every single day of your life. Hannah told me to give them a smile, but it felt so strange. I cringed when I later came across the picture on Google – it looks as if I'm gurning!

In the car on the way to the police station, Hannah explained that Forrest had been arrested on suspicion of abduction and that Gemma had been taken into protective custody in Bordeaux. It turned out that someone had recognised Forrest from one of the pictures that appeared in the press and the police had set a trap for him.

The media presence had felt quite intrusive at times, but I couldn't thank them enough for their help in finding my daughter. I wrote a short statement thanking the press and emailed it to Nick Cloke for his approval.

What I didn't realise at the time, however, was that there were now restrictions on what could be said about the case in the media. As a minor who had potentially been the victim of a sexual crime, Gemma automatically had rights to anonymity. From this point on, the media would not be allowed to reveal her name, or the names of anyone else that could lead to her identity being revealed.

People have asked me why Forrest wasn't charged with 'kidnapping'. That is when a person is taken away by force, while 'abduction' refers to when a minor is taken without parental consent. In this case it was one permission slip that Mr Forrest had neglected to get me to sign ...

Throughout the whole of this book, I have referred to my daughter as Gemma, as this was the name that she had given herself while she was with Forrest in France. She had chosen the name Gemma Grant as it is connected to the real name of her favourite singer, Lana Del Rey. It was also a name that the media picked up on after she and Forrest were found. The press always referred to her as 'Gemma Grant' or the 'Runaway Schoolgirl'.

Unfortunately for me, Nick Cloke said that I couldn't contact the press to give them my thanks. I would have loved to have had an opportunity to say how grateful I was, but this was out of my hands. For my part, I had only done a press conference to put my own message out to Gemma. After that, it was the media who kept the message alive and helped spread it far and wide.

When we reached the police station in Eastbourne, Hannah took me up to the major incident suite, where I was met by a group of senior police officers with big smiles on their faces.

There was Mark Ling, Neil Ralph and the assistant chief

constable, Robin Smith. Mark jokily said, 'The assistant chief constable wants to take full credit for finding Gemma!' Assistant chief constable Robin Smith was actually a very straight-backed, unassuming man who would never have said anything like that, and the rest of his team thought it was hysterical when I threw my arms round him and gave him a kiss to thank him for everything they had done.

Behind them was a white board headed up with the title Operation Oakwood, which was the name the case had been given – as I was later to learn, the names for police operations, like hurricanes, are chosen alphabetically. It was really interesting to see a police-eye view of the case. The board listed sightings, unconfirmed and confirmed, the possible clothing that Gemma would be wearing and other facts about the search for her.

Hannah, meanwhile, was now on her way to Gatwick, from where she was going to fly to Bordeaux. Mark Ling told me that he would have loved for me to be able to go, too, but there was only one seat left on the plane and Gemma had to be accompanied home by a police officer. While I was disappointed that I couldn't go straight to her, I completely understood.

The next thing that Mark said more than made up for it, though.

'Would you like to speak to your daughter?'

'*Would* I?' He didn't need to ask me twice! And he got straight on the phone and put me through to Gemma.

Mark and the team left me alone to talk to her. 'Hello, sweetheart, are you OK?' I said, then I heard her burst into tears. 'I'm so sorry, Mum ...'

From the moment Gemma had been found, I began to

wonder if she wanted to come home to me. I'd always believed that we had a great relationship, but maybe she didn't want to be with us. I knew I had to ask.

I took a deep breath. 'Do you want to come home?'

She sounded so young and frail, so full of sadness and despair: 'I didn't even want to come here in the first place, I just want to come home.'

Her voice was a sound that I had feared I would never hear again. There was so much that I wanted to say to her, but I was happy just to listen to her, to know she was truly alive and that I wasn't just dreaming. At that point, it was totally irrelevant what had been happening, I was just so happy to know that she was coming back. In any case, I didn't want to overwhelm her with questions after everything she'd been through.

We only spoke for about five minutes, but I explained that a lovely lady called Hannah was on her way over to meet her and bring her back to the UK. I told her that we had got to know Hannah really well and that she had even held Lilly for me. I wanted Gemma to know that she could trust Hannah and that everything would be alright.

I then found myself clicking into 'mum mode', asking her if she'd been eating enough, if she was tired or needed anything, but she said she was OK and that I didn't need to worry any more. It was such a relief to hear her voice.

I could hardly speak because of the grin on my face, but before I ended the call, I made Gemma promise that she wouldn't run away again. I was so confused about what had happened. Who was to say that she wouldn't want to just escape from the drama and run away again?

Mark Ling then asked me if I would like to be introduced to the team who had been working on the case and led me into the main operations room. I couldn't believe the scale of it. There were at least 30 officers behind their desks and they all started clapping and cheering as I walked in. It was just incredible. On the walls there were more white boards, each with much more detailed information on them, showing what a huge operation it had been. I was awestruck by how many people had been involved and the amount of work it had taken to find Gemma.

Completely blown away, I made up a little speech on the spot, thanking them for everything they had done. I said that words couldn't actually express how grateful we all were for how much support and care we had all received from them. I added that I hoped we hadn't been too demanding and joked that the only thing I had ever asked of an officer was a cigarette! One of the officers stepped forward and said, 'If it's a fag that you want, then that's what you shall have!' They were all so lovely to me and it was so nice to be able to smile and joke around with them. It was such a contrast to the nightmare that I'd been through over the previous seven days.

A group of about five of us went outside for a cigarette together. 'It's so fantastic to have her back,' one of the police officers told me. 'Tonight will be the first time in a long while that I have been able to tuck my children up in bed.' It really hit me very deeply to see how many other people had been affected by what had happened.

Next, I met up with Jim, the family liaison officer who had helped us over the weekend when Gemma first went missing. It was lovely to see him at the other side of the investigation; it felt like the whole episode had gone full circle. Jim introduced me to Sarah, the family social worker, and they explained to me what was going to happen next.

There had been some stories in the media saying that Gemma would be taken into care when she returned to England. The reports had really upset me because they seemed to me to be suggesting that I must have been a terrible mother for letting this kind of thing happen to my daughter in the first place.

Jim reassured me that this wasn't the case at all. Gemma was being kept in protective custody while she was in France to keep her safe while she was there, but she would come straight home to the family as soon as she returned to England. There was no question that the social services were going to take her away from us.

Sarah told us that the Children's Services department had arranged a safe house in the country for us so that we could all lie low for a few days. It would give us time to regroup and would keep the press at bay.

We also discussed what Gemma's state of mind was likely to be after the experience. In order to work out how I was going to handle the situation, Sarah asked me a series of questions and evaluated my responses. She needed to be sure that Gemma wouldn't come home to a barrage of interrogations and demands that she just forget about Forrest and move on with her life. I also needed to be prepared in case Gemma said she was in love and wanted to be with him. It was going to be a challenging time for everyone concerned.

I wanted the whole episode to be over, but I had to be realistic about the situation. My first priority was Gemma. I had a hundred unanswered questions, but I knew that she had to tell me on her own terms. She was fifteen, still a child – still my little girl – and had been through so much. She needed time to process everything that had happened.

Unbeknown to me, Max was giving a press conference

with Jason Tingley at Sussex Police HQ while I was meeting the team in Eastbourne. I only found out about this after the event, but I was glad to be able to go home and breathe.

It was lovely to have a house full of happiness again. Maddie and Lee were there, and we were all enjoying being together as a happy family. There were loads of messages on Facebook from well-wishers and the phone kept bleeping with texts from friends.

Jason Tingley phoned on his way home from the press conference to tell me how happy he was for us. I could hear the elation in his voice. He too has children and I knew he had been deeply touched by the incredible outcome.

Once Paul and I had got Alfie and Lilly tucked up in bed, we sat down together with his parents, who had come up to stay for the weekend. At some point, we switched on the TV and there was a *Sky News* journalist reporting live from outside our house, saying how there were no signs of life inside and that I had flown to France to be reunited with Gemma.

It was so funny. There we were, eating our dinner and watching her live on TV from the other side of our window! Paul begged to put the outside light on and show her that there was someone home, but I was scared it would only make the reporters start knocking on the door again. 'No signs of life, eh?' my father-in-law laughed. 'I'm in here eating my dinner! What more life does she want?' I'm surprised they didn't hear us laughing.

I was so happy – and not even the news that Gemma's biological father Gary had spoken to a newspaper about her disappearance was going to ruin things. Even though she hadn't seen him or spoken to him for several years, he was going on about how upset he was about her going missing. He said he thought she would be sensible and mature about the situation, though I don't know how he could possibly know that as they'd had so little contact over the years.

After all that had happened, I was too exhausted to get wound up, though. The important thing was I knew Gemma was coming home to me.

Finally, I could go to bed and get some proper sleep rather than just passing out, exhausted, on the sofa. I was so excited about seeing Gemma, though I knew I couldn't completely relax until I had her safely in my arms again …

CHAPTER 13

OPERATION
CAR SWITCH

The next morning was crazy as we packed bags in preparation for our mystery tour to the safe house in the country.

Max and I agreed that Alfie should stay with him while we were away; he often stayed with his dad and we felt it would be too confusing to upset his routine by taking him off to the country. He had been bewildered enough by all the cars in our street and the strangers that had been coming round, and we wanted everything to be as normal as possible for him.

It was the worst packing I have ever done and I ended up leaving loads of things we needed for Lilly at home. What we packed was really quite random. I didn't have a clue where we were going, or what we would need, and I seemed to have packed loads of one thing and not enough of another. As you may have gathered, my mind wasn't really on what I was doing!

Jim called to explain how the police planned to make sure we weren't followed to the safe house. He would pick me up and drive me to Eastbourne police station, where we would then swap cars and go on to pick up Gemma from Gatwick airport before heading for the safe house. Paul was going to come along later with Lilly, while Chloe would follow on with Lee and Maddie the following day.

Jim came to pick me up and at Eastbourne police station we duly swapped cars. I had to duck down in my seat in case any of the reporters there spotted us. It was so surreal. It was only when we got a few miles away from the station that we felt sure we weren't being followed to the airport.

Meanwhile, Paul was at home with Lilly when all of a sudden he heard car doors slamming out in the road and looked out to see a mass exodus of press speeding off in their cars. They had obviously been tipped off that Gemma was going to be on the flight from Bordeaux that was arriving at Gatwick at 3pm.

I don't know which route Jim and I took to get to Gatwick, but eventually we pulled up at a small building set apart from the main airport terminal. The building was surrounded by armed police officers, and we were taken inside by two smartly dressed hospitality people. They asked if I needed anything and I nervously asked them if I could have a coffee. The next thing I knew I was being served a coffee in a very nice china cup and saucer. I didn't realise that we had actually arrived at the Royal Suite and were getting the full VIP treatment!

We were led into an immaculate reception room with leather sofas, televisions on the walls and tables laden with muffins, sweets and drinks. It looked out on to the tarmac at Gatwick and we were told that it is where the royal family and foreign dignitaries fly out from. Next to that room was another airy room with fresh fruit on the table. It was very smart and spotlessly clean. One of the hospitality people told me that it was always kept ready in case a VIP needed to use it, but they were never informed who the VIP was beforehand for security reasons.

While Jim and I waited for Gemma's flight to arrive, we watched the news on TV and read more of the press coverage of Gemma's story. The *Daily Mail* claimed that Gemma had used my passport, which was completely untrue – she had taken her own passport with her. She subsequently threw it away when she and Forrest arrived in Paris, which meant she had to get special clearance to travel back to the UK without one.

After what seemed like the longest wait, the plane landed and Gemma, accompanied by Hannah and Andy Harbour, was brought to us in a minibus.

The next thing I knew, Gemma was standing there in front of me. She dropped her bag and flung her arms around me, and we both cried as we held each other tightly.

She looked tired and drawn; she felt like a bag of bones and smelt unfamiliar. Although she had only been away for a week, I could see on her face that the stress of it all had taken its toll. She had tried to bleach her hair to disguise herself, but it had gone a bit wrong and it was now a strange orange colour. Her clothes had been taken away for DNA testing, so she was wearing clothes that the British consulate had bought for her. They were a bit too big, which only made her look even thinner.

I felt so sorry for her and was so incredibly relieved to have her back.

Switching into mum mode again, I asked her if she had eaten. She told me the first proper meal she had been able to eat was the night before with Hannah and Andy Harbour, who had been looking after her. Hannah had shared a room with her and Andy had kept knocking on the door throughout the night to check she was still there. They were under strict instructions from Mark Ling to make sure she didn't run away again and Hannah even made sure to sleep by the window in case she decided to try and make an escape. As a result, none of them had slept very well and they all looked completely exhausted.

Meanwhile, the press were waiting in the arrivals hall at the airport, ready to capture our tearful reunion for tomorrow morning's newspapers. What they didn't know, of course, was that we were at a different part of the airport, from where we could quickly get away unnoticed.

Once we were in the car and on our way to the safe house, I decided that it would be a good time to let Gemma know that her story had been in the press 'quite a bit' – I didn't want her to get a shock when she saw the headlines. I asked her if she had seen anything about their story in France, but she said she hadn't been paying attention to French newspapers or TV. She said Forrest had spotted a small news bulletin about them having gone missing when they had visited an internet café, but nothing more.

At that very moment, a news report came on the radio saying that Gemma would be returning to England that afternoon. I remember the expression on her face as the penny dropped and she realised that the story was much bigger than she thought.

After a 45-minute drive, we pulled up at a lovely cottage

tucked away from the main road in Tenterden in Kent. It had a small garden that backed on to rolling fields and inside was everything we needed. It felt safe and a million miles away from prying eyes.

As Jim and Hannah left, Paul arrived with Lilly and the hugs and tearful reunions began again. Gemma was so happy to see her baby sister. 'Now, finally, I can begin to relax,' I thought, 'my family is coming back together.'

It was like a heavy weight had been lifted from my shoulders. I knew there would be a lot of tears and heartache to come, but all that mattered was that Gemma was safe.

Gemma wanted to sleep in the same bedroom as me and so that night we pulled the two twin beds together and cuddled up. She proceeded to pour out her heart to me about what had happened in France. I didn't ask her to elaborate or start interrogating her, I just allowed her to talk and talk and talk until the early hours of the morning, and she fell asleep in my arms.

I have never told anyone what Gemma said to me that night, and I swore to her then that I never will. A lot of the facts came out in the subsequent court case, but much of that night's conversation was about her innermost thoughts and feelings. It is a moment that I will always treasure.

The following morning, Lee and Maddie arrived with Chloe. I was worried that the kids would tell Gemma too much about what had been going on while she was away, or bombard her with questions, but they were really respectful and caring about how she would be feeling. They were so happy to have their sister back and just started up the usual sibling banter, taking the mickey about her hair colour and talking about general teenage stuff. We missed Alfie not being with us, but it made me so happy to see them all bickering again like normal brothers and sisters.

CHAPTER 14

TIME TO REFLECT

I was finding it hard to process what Gemma had told me the night before. It was going to take me a long time to come to terms with what I had heard.

Chloe could tell that I was troubled and asked me what had happened. She didn't pry – she never has – but she wanted me to know that she was there for me if I ever needed a shoulder to cry on. The whole situation was so strange. We all just had to try to deal with things the best we could and move forward at our own pace.

A little while later, Jim came over to take DNA swabs from Gemma's mouth, after which Hannah and Sarah came over to interview her. When they were in France, Hannah had asked Gemma if the police could examine her, but she had refused, which she had every right to do. As it was, it turned out that an examination wasn't vital because the police had found so much incriminating DNA evidence on her and Forrest's clothing, but I assured Hannah and Sarah that I would get Gemma checked over with our GP and the sexual health clinic.

There was so much for Gemma to take in. Paul had brought a huge pile of newspapers with him, and over the next few days she pored over every single one of them.

Gemma was shocked at how the story had spread and how the press had spun it, and became frightened at how she had suddenly become public property. She couldn't take it all in. Imagine being an ordinary schoolgirl one day and then world news the next. It was a completely overwhelming experience.

She tried to get in touch with Louise, but got no reply. Frustrated, she tried again and again, and finally she got a text message back. As before, though, it had clearly been scripted by Louise's mum. It didn't sound like Louise at all.

Understandably, Gemma was really upset. She missed Forrest terribly and believed that he loved her and that they should – and would – be back together, but she couldn't talk to her best friend about it.

I wanted to scream to Gemma, 'Don't you realise what a monster he is for what he did to you?' But I knew that wouldn't help matters. As she spoke to me, I had to try to make sure I reacted as if she was talking about any other boyfriend. Of course I wasn't pretending it was the best news ever, but I had to strike the right chord. I needed to be someone she could trust and had to try and be realistic about the situation.

When Gemma was missing, I spent the entire time hoping Forrest truly cared about her and would look after her. When I saw pictures of him, I wanted to believe that he was a good man and wouldn't harm her. If Gemma had been an adult and had met someone fifteen years older than her, I would probably have been a bit disappointed, but I would have accepted it. This was different, though. He was her teacher and had a duty of responsibility. She was only fourteen years old when they began their relationship.

It didn't help that some people on the internet – particularly in the comments sections of newspaper stories – were describing it as some kind of modern-day Romeo-and-Juliet story, completely overlooking the fact that he was her school teacher and she was only fourteen when they got together. Not only had Forrest crossed the line, he had broken the law and destroyed her childhood.

Gemma kept saying, 'He's not like that. If you knew him, you would understand', and bit by bit she began to tell me how their relationship had developed, how they had got to know each other through the various after-school clubs that she was involved in, and how the two of them had gone on to spend time together.

Louise and Ben would often provide alibis for the two of them to meet up. When I dropped Gemma at Louise's house, for example, she would stay there for five minutes and then be picked up by Forrest, who would then drop her back at Louise's fifteen minutes before I was due to pick her up. And the days when Gemma had gone to Brighton with Ben … Yes, she had travelled there with Ben, only to spend the day with Forrest.

Then there were the times when she was supposedly staying overnight at Louise's. One time, soon after Lilly had been born, I needed her to go shopping for me as I had to rest after my C-section. It was coming up to Father's Day and I wanted to get a present for Paul from Lilly; it was going to be his first

Father's Day as a dad himself and I wanted it to be special for him. At the time, I thought Gemma was at Louise's, and I rang and rang her. When she eventually called back, she was really flustered and kept tripping herself up with what she was saying.

She later told me that she had been with Forrest that day – and there were several other incidents, too.

Louise and Ben knew all about their relationship and were completely caught up in the romance of it all. I didn't blame them – they were kids after all. They knew what they were doing wasn't right, but they didn't want to betray their friends.

Forrest was such a good manipulator that he had convinced Louise and Ben that they were all friends together, that somehow the teacher–pupil relationship didn't apply to them. He was an educated man and must have known how much of a risk he was taking. I later heard rumours that Gemma wasn't the first to have fallen for his charms.

The time that we all had together at the safe house in Tenterden was important to us; it was precious family time away from all the madness of the press. For three days, we laid low, playing board games and trying to relax. It was great to be 'normal' again.

I must admit, though, I still felt a bit paranoid. The whole time I kept the curtains drawn in the rooms at the front, and I was a bit wary when I met the woman who lived next door, convinced she must know who we were. I even hid from the people on horses when they rode past the cottage. It was madness, I know, but I really wasn't myself.

We were meant to be staying at the cottage until the Wednesday, but we decided to leave on the Tuesday night. If there were any reporters still hanging around outside our house back in Eastbourne, there would be less chance of them being there if we got back late, we reckoned.

Luckily, the coast was clear when we got back. We were able to unload the car easily and, finally, make ourselves at home again.

CHAPTER 15

CHALLENGING SUBJECTS

Gemma took one look at her bedroom and said: 'I'm not sleeping there!'

She was adamant. For a start all her things seemed to be in different places since the police had searched it, but more than anything it just had too many memories for her. In fact, she never slept in that room again.

Tucked up on the sofa in her pyjamas, my little girl looked so scared and vulnerable. I was so relieved to have her home again, but I was still worried that she might try and run away to be near Forrest. 'Please don't run away again,' I pleaded with her. She looked at me sadly before saying, 'I've got no reason and nowhere to run away to …'

On the Wednesday, Gemma was due to be interviewed by officers at a police house in Hailsham. Before we set off, I asked how she had slept, and she told me she'd had nightmares all night. Later I found out what they were about and I'm not surprised in the slightest that she was disturbed.

When Forrest was arrested, Gemma was seized by plain-clothes policemen, dressed in black. Not knowing who they were, she panicked, thinking she was being kidnapped. Kicking and screaming to try and get away, the policemen had been quite forceful with her. The whole experience had been extremely traumatic for her, particularly on top of everything that she had already gone through. Little wonder she was haunted by what had happened.

The police house was a really odd place. Downstairs it was like any other normal house, but upstairs there was a medical room and a soundproof room with cameras and recording devices. It is used in cases where it is deemed that it would not be suitable to use a regular interrogation room – when, for example, the police are interviewing a minor or a vulnerable victim. Gemma ticked both of those boxes.

While Gemma was being interviewed upstairs I stayed downstairs. I thought it would take an hour or so, but the session ended up lasting seven hours. She was allowed comfort breaks, of course, but the poor thing had to endure hours and hours of questioning. All I wanted to do was put my arms around her and take her out of the situation, but I couldn't. 'I'm sorry, sweetheart, I know this is awful for you,' I told her, 'but there are questions that need to be asked.'

The police wanted to know every single detail about how she had met Forrest, and how their relationship developed. Trouble was, what she revealed in those initial interviews was completely different from what she was later to say in court.

At the time, she wasn't focussing on anyone's negative opinions about her relationship with Forrest. Swept up in the romance of it all, she couldn't understand why it was such a big issue. She was very frank and honest about what had happened. As far as she was concerned, it was a love story, pure and simple. She felt mature enough to make her own decisions in life and was frustrated that people couldn't understand that.

For my part, I was torn. I knew she loved Forrest, but I wanted her to understand that he had crossed the line. Whatever she thought of him, he had a duty of care as her teacher. He knew that he was breaking the law.

It was to take a while for her to realise that Forrest was not all he seemed. At the time, she was too much in love with him and totally wrapped up in the romance of it all. In her eyes, she didn't see that there was any problem and had no idea about the true depth of his manipulation.

The police also discovered that Forrest had allegedly been seeing other women while he was having the relationship with Gemma. Amazingly, I believe his wife Emily never suspected a thing.

I heard rumours about a girl who worked in a pub in Bristol and another woman in London he was allegedly having an affair with. As far as Emily was concerned, he was just heavily involved in school activities and various further education courses. She had no idea that anything untoward was going on.

Forrest had told Gemma that he and Emily had stopped having a physical relationship. Again, though, he wasn't telling the truth. Yes, there had been arguments between them, but they were working on their marriage to fix it.

I so wanted to believe Gemma for her own sake, but meanwhile, the evidence was stacking up against Forrest.

CHAPTER 16

'NORMALITY'

The first couple of weeks after Gemma came back were a bit of a blur. There was so much to deal with in terms of police visits, questioning, counselling, forms to fill in and just trying to get back to normal.

It was incredibly difficult under the circumstances. For a start, our house had become a sort of freak-show tourist attraction. Total strangers would walk down the street and peer in through the windows. It was as if we were Fred and Rose West – people were having a day trip to see the freaky family.

I felt so sorry for our neighbours; they had to endure so much disruption when the media descended on the street. Some of them didn't know what to say when they saw us. We had lived there for 10 years and had a really good relationship with the ones we knew, but all of a sudden there was so much awkwardness. I wanted to say, 'It's OK, you can still talk to us. We can talk about the weather, if you like – anything is fine.'

Everything seemed to be such a challenge to get through. On Thursday, 3 October, Gary, Gemma's biological father, was in the papers again. I went online and there it was: a great big picture of him and this message to his daughter: 'I love her very much, I am so glad she is safe. I'd also like to say that I am not angry with her at all – we all do silly things when we are young without thinking about the consequences.'

My sister Annette phoned Gary's mum and asked her to stop him talking to the press as it was really stressing Gemma out. His mum said she was only concerned about her grandchildren and seemed very unimpressed with her son's behaviour, although she was too loyal to him to say so.

The next time he appeared in the papers, Annette called his mum again and left a message. She never called back, but that was the last time Gary was in the press, so I think she must have stepped in and told him to stop. It's a shame, but we are not in touch with Gary's mum at all now because of this. We used to try and stay in contact, but because of my relationship with Gary, it was too difficult for us to maintain our friendship.

On a more positive note, things were starting to move forward, and on Thursday, 4 October I opened the curtains for the first time in weeks. My next-door neighbour Katrina said it was so nice to see, that it was sign that, finally, things were starting to get back to normal.

Back at home, Gemma continued to refuse to sleep in her bedroom. We had already been thinking about moving, but now it had become a matter of urgency.

I met up with a woman called Lucy from Eastbourne

Borough Council, who explained all our options. I loved the house that we were in and liked our neighbours – even if relationships were slightly strained now – but we needed more space for everyone. Besides, with disturbing letters in the post and strange cars or people standing outside, plus the memories of Gemma's room being searched, it didn't feel like home any more. We had to stay in the same area, though, so that we could be in the catchment area for Sussex Police and Alfie could stay on at his school. Lee and Maddie were petrified but I needed to keep stability in their lives. Emotionally it was incredibly tough but I never kept them in the dark and always gave them options. They were incredible though; they fronted it all and dealt with it. Lucy explained that we could rent somewhere privately, buy with shared ownership or buy outright, but none of the places we saw were quite right. We eventually moved into a new place five months later, but it was a long haul before we got there.

While we were trying to get things back to normal, Gemma tried again to get in touch with Louise and Ben. I knew the two of them really well, of course, but I didn't know much about their parents – other than the fact that they had obviously brought up their children well, as they were such nice kids. So I was a bit surprised when Ben said that he would come over, and then proceeded to bring his mum along with him – I suppose she wanted to check out what kind of woman I was. I felt totally under the spotlight the whole time she was there; it was very disturbing. I've always prided myself in bringing up my children the best way I possibly can, but it was almost as if she was blaming me for what had happened to Gemma. She wasn't the only one, of course. There was plenty of character assassination going on about me on social media.

A similar thing happened with Louise. Although Gemma hadn't been able to speak to her when we were in the safe house, her mum called me when we were back, saying she wanted the girls to carry on seeing each other. First, though, she wanted to meet me. She was really nice and we got on very well. She told me how the case had affected their family and how angry and upset Louise's dad had been about everything that was going on. I felt so bad for them. She was lovely about the whole situation, but regretfully Louise's dad would only let the girls see each other if they had supervised visits.

We tried to make it work, but it was just too awkward. Louise's mum tried to give them space when Gemma visited, but there was just too much water under the bridge for their friendship to survive. Louise was really upset that she had been put in a position where she'd had to lie to the police, and some of her classmates had been accusing her of hindering the investigation. Whereas before Gemma could confide everything about her love for Forrest, the terms 'child abuse' and 'abduction' had tainted the romance. Their friendship just fell apart.

It was another sadness to add to the list. Not surprisingly, Gemma felt very much alone. She had lost her boyfriend and best friend within the space of a few days. There was so much for her to contend with.

I wasn't coping well either; I had suffered from panic attacks when I was with Gary, and once again stress started taking over. I became obsessed with what everyone else was saying about me on social media. It got to the point where I would read it long into the night. Paul was frustrated and worried by how it was affecting me, so I started going online in secret, sometimes even while I was in the bathroom.

I remember one day I was cleaning the living room and *This Morning* was on in the background. There I was, polishing the table when Phillip Schofield and Holly Willoughby started talking about Gemma's case with their guests, radio presenter Nick Ferrari and anti-knife crime campaigner and actress Brooke Kinsella. Brooke was speculating on what it must be like for me as a parent and I started talking to the TV, saying, 'Yes, you're right!' She seemed to be one of the few people who could see sense. It was so bizarre that famous people were talking about me on TV and there I was, watching it and answering back!

I was paranoid that everyone had an opinion about me as a parent, that they were watching my every move. One day, I went shopping in Sainsbury's with Gemma and I became convinced that we'd been recognised. My heart started palpitating, my head was pounding and my hands were sweaty. I had to get out of there so I just grabbed a few things, paid and left.

It scared the hell out of me that I was starting to have panic attacks again. My health had begun to suffer from the moment Gemma had disappeared. My left eye was twitching due to lack of sleep and I started getting migraines; my hair was starting to thin and my Caesarean scar wasn't healing as quickly as it should have been. I had no appetite; I was totally rundown.

I started having nightmares that Forrest would escape and come and get Gemma. In my dreams I would have visions of him with his hand over her mouth, dragging her through the front door, and would wake up in hot sweats. I would double- and triple-check that the door was locked, but I couldn't stop the recurring nightmare.

It got to the stage where I was afraid to go to sleep. Now I was operating on autopilot, trying to deal with the kids, the home, appointment after appointment. I went on feeling that way for so long that it actually felt 'normal' after a while. I only got a chance to speak to the doctor about it the following February – she offered me some sleeping tablets, but I was too scared to take them in case I couldn't wake up if there was an emergency in the house. Totally exhausted, I just wandered around in a daze all the time.

Some time later, when Forrest was being held in Lewes Prison, I thought it might help me sleep better if I researched how many breakout attempts there had been and I wanted to visit the place to check out its security. I just couldn't bear the idea of Forrest laying his hands on my daughter again. The police assured me that he wouldn't be able to escape, so that was one thing – just about – that I could stop fretting over.

I had promised the social worker that I would get Gemma checked out at a sexual health clinic. On the day we went there, I remember whispering to the receptionist, 'Please don't say her name out loud', because I was so paranoid that we would be recognised by others in the clinic. Under any other circumstances, I wouldn't normally have batted an eyelid, but after all that had happened it just added to my paranoia.

Gemma's personality started to change, too. Normally so friendly and open, it got to a stage where she wouldn't talk to anyone. I persuaded her to see Ben, but after an hour-and-a-half, she called me to go and pick her up. It wasn't that he was telling her that she needed to move on or anything – he was still caught up in the romance of their story at the time – she just couldn't handle being away from home.

She was extremely hurt and upset for me when the internet

trolls started picking on me, ripping me to shreds about how rubbish I was as a mother and making cruel comments about my appearance. On YouTube, for example, under the video of the police press appeal that Max and I did, one of the comments picked up on the fact that I have a gap in my teeth. They wouldn't have known, of course, but it was caused by a lack of calcium during pregnancy. A little further down, someone else commented, 'Cue Jeremy Kyle', as if we were some terrible family just hungry for fame.

It was all so cruel. I never chose to be in the limelight. I'm not a celebrity who looks like a model, just an ordinary mum trying to do the best for my kids. Yet no matter how incredibly hurtful the things people wrote about me were, for some reason I couldn't stop myself from reading them. It became an addiction; I needed to know everything about the case.

I was also determined to find out everything I could about Forrest. When Gemma first disappeared, I only wanted to know that he wouldn't harm my daughter and that he really did love her. I blocked out what he had done sexually to my child. Rightly or wrongly, it was the only way that I could handle the situation.

Once Gemma was back, though, I wanted to know more about him. Who was this monster who had come into our lives and ripped our world apart?

Paul also wanted answers; he never got as obsessed as I did but his whole world was affected by this man we knew nothing about.

One day, when we had been back home for a few weeks, I told Paul that I wanted to get out of the house for the evening. I didn't care where we went or what we did, I just needed a change of scenery. Little did I know, but in the back of his mind, he'd had exactly the same idea as me about where we should go …

When we got into the car and he asked me where I wanted him to drive, he wasn't in the slightest bit surprised when I said 'Ringmer', which was where Forrest had lived. It was about a 15-minute drive and I remember when we got there, I was disappointed at how lovely it was. Forrest had been there with Gemma and I had hoped it would be horrible and seedy, just as his crime had been. Instead, it was a lovely leafy village with a village green, little shops and country pubs. It was a real gem of a place. Ironically, it was the kind of place that I would have liked to move to, had I been there before. Now, though, it would be forever tainted by his crime.

Paul and I had no idea which street he lived in and spent an hour or so driving around before giving up for the night. Of course, Gemma would have known exactly where he lived, but we weren't about to ask her – it would have totally freaked her out.

That night, we sat in bed and studied an online map. The newspapers had published photographs of his house and given the name of the road where he lived, and the next day, Paul and I set off to Ringmer again. We parked on the other side of the road to his house and just stared at it. This might sound weird, but just by looking at it, it helped us piece more of the jigsaw together. It was a very nice house and Forrest was obviously financially very comfortable. What was sad was that all of the windows had been papered over, presumably by his wife. Clearly we weren't the only ones who'd had to adapt to a different kind of life because of what Forrest had done.

We still had the press hanging around our house – we had even become sort of used to it – but there was no sign of any press here. Forrest's wife had moved away soon after the scandal had hit. Now the house was just a shell of the home it used to be.

CHAPTER 17

FORREST RETURNS

As quickly as we were trying to adjust to life as a family again, over in France the wheels had been set in motion to get Forrest back. On Tuesday, 2 October, he appeared in court in Bordeaux for the first time.

The European arrest warrant stipulated that he was to be extradited to the UK charged with abduction. However, the Crown Prosecution Service was determined to add an extra charge of sexual activity with a minor; the police were confident they had enough evidence to support both charges.

Forrest didn't contest the charge of child abduction and said he was happy to be extradited to England, claiming, 'I am keen for everyone to know the truth.'

When I heard about this statement, I was confused. Was there something I didn't know? Detective Inspector Neil Ralph assured me that there was nothing I hadn't been told, and I assumed Forrest was just showboating for the media. Surely he didn't have a hope of getting away with his crimes? All the evidence was stacked against him.

Forrest had hired a team of hotshot lawyers – I later discovered that they specialise in getting celebrities off potential charges on technicalities – and a French barrister to act on his behalf in court. While he seemed happy to be extradited to face the charge of abduction, his legal team challenged the second charge of sexual activity with a minor. They claimed it was unlawful to add an extra charge to the original European arrest warrant, so the court was adjourned.

Later, after hearing the cases for and against the Crown Prosecution Service's position, the judge agreed that the additional charge of sexual activity with a minor could be added. No sooner did he allow it, though, than Forrest's legal team appealed, meaning the case was then referred to the European Court of Justice in Luxembourg.

We were baffled – we couldn't understand why Forrest's team were dragging things out like this. Surely there was no way they seriously thought he was going to get away with what he had done? We all knew he was guilty.

I suppose, of course, time was money for the lawyers – they were probably rubbing their hands in glee at the prospect of such a high-profile case. I'd been told Forrest had substantial savings and I suspect his parents helped him out financially, too, as I understood they were financially very comfortable, so perhaps legal costs weren't an issue.

After going back and forth to court, Forrest was finally extradited to England on Wednesday, 10 October. That night, Hannah got in touch to warn me that the press had taken over streets around the court in Eastbourne and she was concerned they might start pestering us at home again. Paul was working away overnight so I packed a bag for the children and me, and we went and hid at Mum's place, which is ten minutes away, for the night.

Forrest was taken to Eastbourne police station, and on Thursday, 11 October he appeared at Eastbourne Magistrates' Court, where he was duly charged with child abduction and remanded in custody. The police requested to keep him at Eastbourne for a further three days in order that they could carry out further investigations.

He did not enter a plea of guilty or not guilty, and did not even mention a bail request. I was surprised about this. Previously I had been worried that he might have been granted bail, but it turned out that he had been advised not to even ask.

It was at this hearing that an Order banning Gemma's real name from being used in the press was imposed under the Children and Young Persons Act 2008. All of the other restrictions regarding publishing pictures of her or identifying any family members were also put in place.

I was told that Forrest's parents came to visit him while he was being held at Eastbourne, but apparently his wife Emily didn't want to know. The police also informed me that he had refused to say a word to them. They asked him all manner of questions about what had happened, but he wouldn't confirm or deny anything. I couldn't help wondering if there was something else up his sleeve that would later come out in court.

Back at home, Gemma was reading online reports about what was happening with Forrest, but she wouldn't talk to me about it. She was still very much under the illusion that she was part of some famous love story. Neil Ralph and Sarah continued to share information with her that Forrest hadn't been quite so faithful to her as he had insisted, but she refused to believe them. As far as she was concerned, it was all lies.

She was desperate to visit him in prison and said that nobody had the right to stop her. I had to be firm and told her she couldn't because she was the victim of the case. And she hated that word. She certainly didn't see herself as a victim – Forrest was her boyfriend and that was that. Gemma wrote to him, but the prison authorities would have intercepted the letters. She was heartbroken about it, but there was no way that she could be allowed to have any contact with him.

I had to shoulder all of her tears, tantrums and anger. Some of the things that Gemma said to me would have been unforgivable had she been anyone other than my child, but I took it all on the chin. I tried to reason with her and kept her informed of absolutely everything I knew regarding the case. Also, I left the door open for her to contact the police and the social services in the hope that they would make her understand that there was a very valid reason why she and Forrest couldn't have any contact, but she didn't want to speak to them.

The fact that Forrest had left his wife and his whole life in England so that they could be together seemed to mean everything to Gemma. When she was with him in France, she loved the fact that they were out holding hands in public rather than having illicit meetings in secret. To her, there was nothing questionable about their relationship.

When I saw the CCTV pictures of Gemma and Forrest together, she appeared happy and confident. In a way, I had found that reassuring because it showed that she wasn't frightened about being with him. But no matter how she felt about him, and even though I knew it was making her terribly unhappy, there was no way she could be allowed to have any contact with him.

CHAPTER 18

THE NEED TO TALK

A week after that seven-hour interview at the police house in Hailsham, Gemma announced that she had more information that she wanted to share with the police. I didn't press her about what this information was, I just duly went along with her.

It turned out that she was starting to get angry about what she was hearing about Forrest's past. She wanted to tell the police that she wouldn't have started any relationship had she known he was still having a relationship with his wife. She isn't that type of person and she had believed everything he had told her. She didn't add anything that would support the evidence the police already had, but she took the opportunity to express her feelings. The interview lasted five hours and I wouldn't say she felt better afterwards by any means. She was confused and hurt, and the one person she could ask for confirmation in all of this was in prison.

On one hand, social media was saying she was part of an amazing love story. On the other, she was being told 'lies' about her boyfriend. She wanted a chance to put the record straight about the love they had for each other. As before, she once again insisted it wasn't an infatuation, it was real.

I had hoped the interview would reveal more information, but it didn't. The police were very understanding, however. They wanted Gemma to feel comfortable to be able to speak to them.

At home, things were starting to be fractious between us. I was trying to monitor what Gemma was eating and drinking, and how much sleep she was getting, but I also had to give her plenty of space. She was very defensive if anyone was horrible about me on social media, but there was an increasingly bigger barrier growing between us. Quite honestly, I didn't know how to deal with it.

Sarah, the family social worker, had been absolutely brilliant with all of us. Gemma was already having sessions with a therapist, and Sarah suggested that the rest of the family should get some counselling as well. It would be a safe, controlled environment allowing us all to speak freely about our feelings. This could only be positive, right?

It ended up backfiring really badly. We were only a couple of sessions into our therapy when Gemma and Lee took it upon themselves to annihilate me as a mother. It was just an onslaught of the most horrible things. They claimed that I had got together with Paul too quickly after splitting up with Max and that we had decided to have a baby together without thinking it through. They also said I had been working so hard and didn't have enough time for them.

It was all my fault.

I couldn't believe what I was hearing. We are the type of family that regularly has family conferences if any of us has something on our mind. When I first met Paul, I made sure that I told the children all about him before I allowed them to meet, and we talked about the two of us having a baby with the rest of the children, as a family.

All these allegations from Gemma and Lee were completely new to me. I wanted the ground to open up and swallow me. It was a completely venomous attack.

I remember leaving the session feeling totally shell-shocked. No one said a word in the car on the way home.

I was distraught. When I told Sarah about what had happened, she said she wasn't surprised at all. She told me that they obviously had so much anger about the way their worlds had been torn apart that they had to deflect it on to someone – and I was a safe person for them to release their feelings on.

As their mother, there was no way that I was going to stop loving them for what they said to me. There would never be any consequences about what they said and I would never throw it back at them, so in a way I was the natural target. Sarah said it was part of the process that they were going through, but maybe it had been too soon to start counselling. It was still all just too raw.

And Sarah was right. When I speak to Gemma and Lee about those meetings now, they are full of remorse and find it extremely difficult to talk about what happened.

Meanwhile, the local education authority was concerned

about the amount of school that Gemma was missing – especially as it was her GCSE year – so it was arranged for Gemma, Sarah and me to meet someone from the East Sussex Department of Education. What they proposed astounded me.

They said that the best way forward for Gemma would be for her to return to Kennedy High School, arguing that she needed to reconnect with her old friends and teachers, and that it would be the easiest way for her to get back to her studies. I couldn't believe it. 'Over my dead body! If I allow her to go back to Kennedy High School, it would be like feeding her to a pack of wolves!' I declared.

I hadn't disagreed with anything the police or the Child Protection Services had suggested before this, but there was no way I was going to let that happen.

Amazingly, Gemma wanted to go back to Kennedy High School and said she would not be prepared to go to any other senior school in the area. As far as she was concerned, it would all blow over once the initial curiosity had worn off.

Luckily, there was another option – FLESS, which stands for Flexible Learning Educational Support Service. It is a stepping stone for secondary school children who have spent time out of school for one reason or another, and was perfectly suited to Gemma's situation. The nearest centre to us was in Seaford, about an hour's round trip away. Gemma would have to be taken and picked up from the school, as that was one of the conditions of attendance. It was quite limited in the amount of subjects it offered on its curriculum, but the school was happy to accommodate anything that she required. They offered Skype sessions, but we agreed that Gemma should go there three days a week from 9am until 3pm, starting in

November. Her attendance would be extended to a full week once she had settled in.

We knew we were in for a long stretch but, bit by bit, it felt like life was getting back on an even keel.

On Monday, 12 November, Forrest appeared in Hastings Magistrates' Court via videolink from Lewes Prison and was given another chance to enter a plea of guilty or not guilty. Once again, he refused. As before, we just couldn't work out what was going on. I didn't understand what he was playing at.

The ongoing complications regarding adding the additional charge of sexual activity with a minor meant there was a chance of there being two separate trials. If this second charge continued to go back and forth through the European appeal courts, as it appeared was going to be the case, it could be years before the nightmare was over for us. The plan was to proceed with the original abduction charge and do everything we could to get through the red tape in time to include the sexual activity with a minor charge at the same trial.

We could be facing years with this heavy burden upon us, but all the evidence I had seen had convinced me beyond any shadow of a doubt that Forrest was a sex offender. He had to pay for his crime, and I had to find a way to get my family through all of this.

CHAPTER 19

I WANT ANSWERS

After what Gemma had been through, I wanted answers. Although the school had issued a statement to the press saying that they were supporting our family in every way they could, they barely got in touch with us.

Once we had been back from the safe house for about a week, I requested a meeting with Mr Worship, the executive head of Kennedy High School. Up until now, I had not heard a thing from the school. I went along with a long list of questions. I'd got my daughter back, and she was safe, but now I wanted answers: I needed to know how it had happened in the first place.

To this day, I have never had so much as a phone call from the school's head, Simon Pearl. He answered a couple of my letters, but he has never picked up the phone to speak to me.

First of all, I wanted to know when Mr Worship discovered

what was going on between Gemma and Forrest. He told me he had first heard about the rumours a couple of weeks earlier. I was furious. Wasn't he angry that none of his colleagues had raised the matter with him sooner? I sarcastically said I felt sorry for him that all this was going on under his nose, and asked if he felt bad that he didn't have a good enough relationship with his colleagues for them to have shared what they knew.

I asked to see Gemma's school file – I wanted to see if the information was documented in any way, but I was told I couldn't because it was now part of a criminal investigation. Arguing that I felt it was my right as Gemma's mother to see the file, I explained to him some of the things that my daughter had been coping with since her return. Subsequently, I did get to see some of it.

I also asked him what kind of safeguarding measures were in place for the pupils. I'd searched high and low through all the literature I could find about the school, but there was nothing available. Miraculously, within a day of our meeting, all the information appeared on the school website.

Even though I had previously told Sarah there was no way I was ever going to allow my daughter to go back to that school, she and Mr Worship then started talking about when Gemma should return to Kennedy High School. Over my dead body! I told them in no uncertain terms that the only thing Gemma would be coming back to the school for was her prom in the following June.

And with that, I stormed out.

I was angry with Sarah for siding with Mr Worship. She had got to know us all so well, and she knew the reasons why I felt the way I did about the issue, but she explained that the guideline in cases where pupils had missed a part of their schooling was that they should return to the same school.

Next I went to see Matt Dunkley, the director of child services for East Sussex, and he immediately made me feel really welcome. He said he could totally sympathise with what we had been going through and promised he would do everything in his power to help us. Apparently, Mr Worship had also been in touch with him and had requested an independent review of Kennedy High School's safeguarding policies. Hmm ... I wonder what made him think about doing that?

I told Matt Dunkley that I had been alarmed by the suggestion that Gemma should go back to Kennedy High School and that I was interested in the FLESS option. He assured me that he totally understood how I felt about the situation and agreed with the decision that I had taken.

Matt also told me that a panel had been set up to see if the East Sussex Local Safeguarding Children Board should carry out a serious case review. He explained to me that such reviews normally only happen in cases involving a death, but the circumstances surrounding Gemma's situation were so serious that he felt there was no option but to tackle it this way.

Sometimes you meet someone who is so genuinely on your side it takes the weight of the world off your shoulders while you are with them. Matt Dunkley was one of those people.

Following this we were put in touch with Matt's colleague, Douglas Sinclair, the head of child safeguarding in East Sussex. I wanted to find out more about the training that teachers received – in particular, whether they received guidance about crossing the line with pupils – and he patiently explained to me the process regarding the serious case review.

Another day, another meeting. This time I met up with Iain

Luxford, East Sussex County Council's head of media, who talked me through the implications of the press reporting. To be honest, I hadn't taken a lot of interest in the Leveson Inquiry before that, and he explained to me how flimsy the laws were surrounding reporting.

As a result of all this, I have become very sussed about privacy laws. In the case of celebrities, they choose to have a public life; to some extent that is what they have signed up for. But for innocent people like the family of Milly Dowler, it is just disgusting. People have asked me if I was ever tempted to contact the Dowlers or the parents of Madeleine McCann, but I didn't want to make things any more public. I wanted to contain our situation as best I could and keep a lid on the whole thing. If I could, I would have built a wall around my family and pulled a great big cover down over us.

What with all the meetings, sorting out somewhere new to live and trying to maintain some kind of normality for the children and get life back on track for the rest of the family, those first few weeks after Gemma's return were challenging, to say the least.

Early in November, Gemma began at FLESS in Seaford. I remember her first day there so vividly; it was one of the saddest I had to deal with. It was almost like she was a little girl again, climbing the stairs up to 'big school'. Whenever I have taken any of my children for their first day of school I have always felt a little bit sad, as it marks the end of a certain stage of their life. I know it might sound crazy, but as Gemma went up the stone steps at The Old School in Seaford, I couldn't stop the tears streaming down my face as I drove away. I knew in my heart it was all for the best, but I couldn't help myself.

An hour after I dropped her off, I called the school to check she was OK. I needn't have worried, of course – she was fine – but, as always, she was still my little mermaid to me.

I was so angry that Forrest had put Gemma through all this. After all the stress she had endured, she not only had to come to terms with what had happened between them, but now she had to make new friends and adjust to a whole new way of working. I can never forgive him for that.

CHAPTER 20

NEW 'FRIENDS'

Despite all of the traumas that she was going through, Gemma settled into her new FLESS school amazingly quickly. Initially, the manager of the school thought it would be a good idea for her to create a new identity for herself in order to avoid a hundred questions on her first day, but the pretence didn't last long.

As soon as she said, 'Hi, my name is Demi', one of the other pupils said, 'No, it's not! I recognise you from your picture in the papers.' So that was that. The school was quite strict about how it was up to the person how much they wanted to share about themselves, so Gemma decided to tell everyone a bit about who she was and why she was there, and very quickly the novelty wore off. It really wasn't a big deal to everyone else there.

There were only about seven pupils at the school in total.

I don't suppose any of the others had been in the papers recently, but there was a reason why each of them needed to be there rather than a regular school. They, too, just wanted to catch up on their education.

The tutors there were so accommodating about Gemma's situation. They understood that she was likely to need a lot of time off to attend court hearings and other meetings related to the case, and were happy for her to attend school for half-days or have work sent to her at home. There was also the Skype option; it really was flexible learning.

When Gemma settled in so quickly, we all agreed that she should stay on at FLESS until the end of her GCSE year. The only thing that put a spanner in the works was that she would have to take all her exams back at Kennedy High School because of the strict examination conditions. This wasn't exactly ideal, but it was much better than having to return to the school full-time.

Little did we know how much the court case would take over, but for the moment Gemma was happy and settled. After weeks of stress, she could finally move on with her education.

Gemma quickly made new friends at FLESS and really enjoyed her coursework. She had GCSEs to study for, but she was determined to do her best, knuckling down to work and exceeding everybody's expectations. The regular reports we got from the school said that she was responsible, articulate and mature, and she was very friendly with everyone.

There was a lovely atmosphere there. One particular teacher, Jess, formed a great bond with her and even brought Oreo biscuits into class when she heard that Gemma liked them, while the wife of another teacher would bake cakes for her husband to bring into his lessons. Gemma made some really strong friendships while she was there. All the pupils and teachers seemed to take everyone's reasons for being there in their stride.

At home, though, things hadn't got easier for any of us: there were still so many people coming to the house on an almost daily basis. There was meeting after meeting with the police and social services, not to mention extended family wanting to visit. Gemma didn't want to see anyone. I don't think she was being difficult, she was just embarrassed about all the fuss that she had caused.

She was hooked on social media sites like Facebook and Twitter. She hated reading all the nasty things the trolls were saying about us, but she was also starting to get caught up with people who were trying to befriend her and manipulate her.

There were two women in their thirties who were particularly creepy – actually, to be honest, downright sick would be a better way to describe them. One of them was from the north of England and had created a 'Gemma and Jeremy shrine' on her Facebook page, complete with hearts, stars and flowers all around it. She had Photoshopped pictures of the two of them together in a heart shape and wrote: 'This shrine will not be removed until Jeremy is free.' Even though she had grown-up children of her own, she got unhealthily wrapped up in Gemma's story.

I was also very worried about a woman from Hertfordshire who had got in contact with Gemma. She was even more disturbed than the 'shrine woman'. It was almost as if she had made it her job to make herself part of Forrest and Gemma's 'love story'. She tried to befriend me, Gemma, Forrest's family and our family and friends by pretending she had family connections to all of us.

This woman even created a Facebook account under a different identity in order to contact me and give me parenting advice, telling me how I couldn't control Gemma's feelings, and how she was able to totally sympathise with what Gemma was going through because she too had once had a relationship with her teacher.

And there was worse to come. The 'parasite from Hertfordshire', as I started to call her, started writing to Forrest in prison and even went to visit him. This would have meant a round trip of around four hours and yet, all the time she was visiting him, this wicked woman's husband didn't have a clue what was going on. She promised Forrest that she would support him and look after Gemma until he was freed, then they could be together again. How twisted is that?

Another day, I received an unusually large bill for Gemma's phone, which was in my name. Concerned, I asked the phone company to provide me with an itemised list of the calls that had been made and, on checking it, noticed that almost every single one was to the same number. I didn't recognise who the number belonged to and so, naturally, I called it. I now know that it was the parasite from Hertfordshire. I asked who she was and, cool as anything, she replied: 'You should know, you called me.' I told her I had found her number on my daughter's phone bill and ended the conversation with a very forceful 'Stay away from my daughter!'

I became aware of these two nutters very early on, but it was difficult to do anything about it. Of course I talked to Gemma about them and tried to impress upon her that they weren't real friends, they were parasites who had nothing else in their lives and were feeding off the drama. To start off with, I think she just saw them as harmless spectators who shared her love story, but they became more dangerous as they reached out to her, offering her a link to Forrest.

But I was realistic about how much Gemma would tell me. I was a teenager once, too, and there were certain things I never told my mum. I knew she needed an outlet to share her feelings and get things off her chest, but I couldn't bear the thought of these strange women having any kind of hold on my daughter.

I spoke to the police about taking further action against them, but they advised me against it. There was no doubt that these women were warped individuals, but they hadn't actually committed a crime as such. The police were aware of what was being said on social media and had a team of officers monitoring sites such as Facebook and Twitter. They advised me to keep a close eye on the situation and to let them know if I ever suspected that a crime had been committed.

I later discovered that Forrest's mother had joined a couple of the 'Support Jeremy Forrest' pages that had been put up on Facebook and had given the woman operating one of them permission to publish her home address so that people could write to her son. I was disgusted – she seemed to be oblivious to the fact that a lot of these so-called supporters were teenagers caught up in the love story and I felt she was condoning her son's actions. The following Christmas, she even asked the 'supporters' to raise a glass to Forrest at 3pm on Christmas Day so he would know that he had support out there.

One day, I received a call from DI Neil Ralph to tell me that the police had reason to believe that Gemma's email had been hacked. I remember thinking it was probably another of those parasites getting off on Gemma's story, but it turned out to be some geeky nineteen-year-old from Liverpool who obviously just spent too much time online! His poor mum went absolutely mad with him. The boy claimed the reason he had hacked into her files was to help the police with their investigations, though Forrest was already in custody anyway by this time.

The police could have taken legal action, but they decided it wasn't in the best interests of the case. Instead, they made him write a letter of apology to me and Gemma. Besides, as they said, his mother's fury was probably punishment enough.

It chilled me to the bone how much these weird people wanted to be part of Gemma's story. She was at a very impressionable age and yet strangers were grabbing at her like leeches and wouldn't let go.

It was another situation that was out of my control. I kept trying to tell Gemma that these people weren't real friends and didn't care about her feelings, but I was mindful that I couldn't run roughshod over how she was feeling. I knew that the more I pushed her, the more withdrawn she would become. She was incredibly vulnerable and I had to treat her with kid gloves.

Forrest had already damaged Gemma so much and now there was even more for her to deal with. We were all so angry about it and wanted it to stop. I wanted to pick her up and swathe her in bubble wrap. I didn't want to lock her up and stop her having a life of her own, but I wanted Forrest and the parasites to stop getting to her. Like quicksand falling through my fingers, I couldn't keep a hold on the situation and it scared me to death. They kept going on and on at her, and it was to eventually lead to the breakdown of our relationship.

I wasn't the only one who saw how much Gemma's

personality had changed either: Sarah, our family social worker, also did. Gone was the sweet child that I used to know and before me stood a girl who was behaving like an adult. Now I'm not stupid, I never for one minute thought she would stay my little girl forever, but she had started acting like she had an autocue in front of her, telling her what to say when she was asked any questions. It hit me hard to realise that she really had been groomed by a sex offender; Forrest truly had got under her skin.

I knew it wasn't something that I could change overnight. Forrest had known her since she was just thirteen and even if it had been completely innocent, their relationship had been evolving for several years so it wasn't something that she would just forget overnight. I couldn't miraculously undo whatever had been going on between them like a piece of bad knitting.

Gemma spent quite a lot of time with Sarah to begin with, but as time went on, she stopped opening up to her. Sarah arranged for her to continue to receive support from members of her team, but she wouldn't trust anyone who said anything negative about Forrest. It was incredibly frustrating. I was desperate for Gemma to confide in a support worker rather than one of those evil parasites who had befriended her.

Meanwhile, she was turning into someone I didn't recognise anymore. She was her usual self in front of other people, but behind closed doors she was breaking down. To be honest, I didn't really know how to cope with it. I started doing some research on victims of abuse to find out how they coped with life after abusive relationships; I needed to know how to deal with the situation.

One of the people I got in contact with was Marilyn Woods, who had set up the child sexual abuse charity Enough Abuse.

We exchanged a few emails, but we never got the chance to meet as every minute of my time seemed to be taken up, especially when I had to go back to work.

Another person whom I considered contacting was the child protection campaigner Lucy Duckworth, who founded the charity See Changes. When Gemma went missing, it was revealed that Lucy had previously contacted the then Secretary of State for Education, Michael Gove, and our local MP, Stephen Lloyd, about the fact that she had been unable to obtain a copy of the child protection policies at Kennedy High School. Her story was picked up by the press and Stephen Lloyd appeared on TV, talking about the school. I was incensed when I heard him describe Kennedy High as 'exemplary'.

I wrote to him, saying how I angry I was that he seemed to be more interested in the school's processes and procedures than the family of one of his own constituents, but I never heard back from him. Lloyd's assistant, Jack Short, got in touch and told me that the media had taken his words out of context, and assured me that he had mentioned Gemma in his statement. Short sent me the statement so I could see for myself, but quite honestly it didn't make up for the fact that the school once more got an easy ride.

Although I was interested to know more about Lucy Duckworth's experiences with the school, I didn't have the energy to fight even more battles at that point. I had enough on my plate at home, not least because my own obsession with Forrest was now starting to get out of hand, too.

When we had found Forrest's house, Paul's curiosity was sated; he knew what he needed to know. But it wasn't enough for me. I wanted to know every little detail about Forrest – what he did every day in prison, how he had become a teacher, what each and every one of his ex-girlfriends was like. I felt that if I could keep on top of the situation, we could move on with our lives.

It was going to be a long haul for Gemma to find a way through all of the emotional upheaval. Friends and family kept telling me that I was holding everything together really well, but it certainly didn't feel like it at the time. I was just trying to do the right thing.

CHAPTER 21

TRYING TO HOLD IT TOGETHER

Alfie and Lilly were too little to know what was going on in our strange household, but I could tell that it was really affecting poor Maddie and Lee. After we returned from the safe house, Maddie moved back in with us and took over Gemma's bedroom, and she was finding it tough at her school (which was not the one that Gemma went to). She was being bullied and had to deal with a constant stream of nasty comments about Gemma.

Luckily, there was a lovely woman called Mrs Dench at her school who helped her with pastoral care. Sue – we were quickly on first-name terms – used to run the 'sanctuary', which was a room where the kids could go to have some quiet time when they needed it. She and I discussed Maddie's situation and she very kindly made a point of keeping me up to speed whenever Maddie was under too much pressure and allowed her as much sanctuary time as she needed. Sue was wonderful with Maddie and her constant email communication with me really reassured me.

Some people have asked me if I changed my parenting style as a result of what happened to Gemma. While I did in certain respects, I was already very protective about my children's safety. I always tried to make sure that I knew where they were and would never allow them to do things like hang around the streets. What happened to Gemma had been beyond my control, although it took me a long time to accept that fact, especially as regards to those incriminating pictures of Forrest that she had on her phone.

After what happened with Gemma, I became a lot more cautious regarding Maddie's male teachers. I asked her to tell me all about them – who they were, how old they were, what they looked like, how many lessons she had with them, etc. I had a real hang-up about the same thing happening to her, and I wanted to make sure that I knew all about them. Poor Maddie thought I was mad – to her, they were all 'so old' – but I couldn't stop myself panicking about it.

Meanwhile, Lee was getting stressed out by how much attention he was getting because of Gemma. His colleagues at the shop where he worked were really respectful of his privacy, but he was often recognised by customers. It wasn't that they bombarded him with questions or anything, but the mere fact that they would say 'Hope your sister is alright' was a constant reminder. When it became too much for him, he was moved to a different department so that he didn't have to deal with the public. His bosses were great, but he wanted his old life back and eventually he applied for a different job.

It was another thing that Forrest had destroyed.

I just wanted the year to be over. It seemed to be one step forward and two steps back all the time. No matter how hard I tried, something else seemed to happen to slap me in the face.

Some time in November, Gemma came running downstairs with her laptop, shouting, 'Look what I've found!' The song that Forrest had written for her had been put up on his SoundCloud account. We had been under the impression that he had no access to any kind of social media while in police custody and couldn't understand how on earth it had suddenly turned up there.

I was as freaked out about it as much as Gemma was and wondered if perhaps some sick individual had set up an account in his name and put it up as some kind of cruel joke. I asked the police to investigate and they got in touch with Forrest's family, who later confirmed that his younger brother had been responsible. A day or so later, his brother tweeted: 'Sorry if I offended by posting my brother's song. My bad.'

A series of tweets then followed, which only added insult to injury. There was a link to a Lana Del Rey song that Gemma and Forrest really liked and a message along the lines of 'For someone special, it was a song that was theirs'. Another followed with a reference to a Jools Holland show featuring Lana Del Rey that was going to be on that night. It had the message: 'You can be sure he will be watching'.

Gemma was tuned into Twitter and the message really hit its target, once more spinning her into confusion. I got straight back in touch with Mark Ling, chief inspector for child protection, to ask if he could stop him. I so wanted to get life back to normal for Gemma and this was just more stress for all of us to deal with.

The police spoke to his father, Jim Forrest, and warned that further action would have to be taken if his younger son persisted in this kind of activity on social media, as it could be seen as intimidating a potential witness. That seemed to do the trick. The account was shut down and things, for a while, went back to 'normal'.

On Monday, 3 December, Forrest appeared at Brighton Magistrates' Court, again by videolink from Lewes Prison, and the case was committed to the Crown Court. As before, Forrest, did not enter a plea. He spoke only to confirm his name, date of birth and address, which was now in Petts Wood in south-east London. From this, I gathered that he and his wife had now separated and that he was using his parents' address.

Another court appearance over and still no answers. It was punishingly slow. Neil Ralph was as surprised as I was about how little things had moved on with the case, but he assured me that there was nothing to worry about because the case against Forrest was so black and white. But I couldn't understand why they felt the need to drag it all out so long; I wondered if it was just for the money and the publicity.

With Christmas coming up, I started making all the preparations for the holidays. Usually I love that time of year and go completely mad with loads and loads of food, the biggest tree we can possibly get and a crazy amount of presents for everyone. I was determined to make it extra-special for Lilly as this would be her first Christmas. I know she was too tiny to appreciate it, but her life hadn't exactly got off to a good start so far. She had suffered with severe reflux when she was born and we almost lost her when she was five weeks old. Paul and I had to attend resuscitation classes to find out what to do in an emergency, and even had to put those skills into practice on one occasion. As if those first few months hadn't been tough enough for her, there was all the Gemma drama, of course, which made me feel I hadn't been totally there for her.

In the end, and probably not that surprisingly, it was the worst Christmas we have ever had. Somehow we all managed to pick up flu viruses – I think we were just exhausted by everything that had been going on over the previous weeks. In some ways, it was good to be forced to take it easy and have a quieter Christmas than we would normally have had. We spoiled the kids rotten as usual, but it was much more low-key. With everything that was going on, we really didn't feel like celebrating.

One of the nicest things to happen was a phone call I received on Thursday, 27 December from Mark Ling, checking that we were all OK. It was lovely to know that the police were still thinking of us. They knew, of course, that things weren't about to get any easier for us as we got closer to Forrest's trial, though.

CHAPTER 22

SCHOOL FOR SCANDAL

Early in the New Year, the 2013 Ofsted report was published, and the results of the November inspection of Kennedy High School were revealed. Kennedy High had previously always achieved an Outstanding rating, but on this occasion it had been downgraded to Good. I was relieved to see that their incompetence had been recognised in some small way.

In addition to the Ofsted inspection, Douglas Sinclair, the head of child safeguarding in East Sussex, visited me to let me know the key findings of a review into Kennedy High School's safeguarding policies that his team had conducted. They had found that while the school had safeguarding policies in place, teachers there had consistently failed to follow the correct processes.

I had sent my children to Kennedy High School because I believed it was the best school in the area. Little did I know what was really happening behind closed doors. Through my own research, I had made a number of, frankly, very disturbing discoveries about the school. In 2009, a supply teacher was jailed for seven years after he admitted grooming two girls and having sex with them, and in March 2012, the school's former chair of governors, Canon Gordon Rideout, was arrested on suspicion of sexually assaulting young people in the late-1960s and early 1970s. In May 2013, Rideout was found guilty of 36 separate offences at Lewes Crown Court and was sentenced to 10 years' imprisonment.

Jeremy Forrest was number three in a colourful history of offenders working at the school.

On top of that, there was a lot of worrying gossip about other members of staff doing the rounds. It had been alleged, for example, that another teacher, who was no longer at the school, had been having a relationship with a girl around the same time as the Forrest–Gemma scandal, but this was never officially confirmed.

I was also told that another teacher had joked about what had happened to Gemma. Apparently, when one of his pupils was being disruptive in class, he said to them: 'If you behave, I'll let you go early, but don't think I'm going to treat you to a trip to France ...'

His sickening words quickly got back to me via friends of Gemma's. Furious, I couldn't believe that he would dare joke about something so disturbing. Of course I wasn't there at the time, so I appreciate that it may well have been that the situation was exaggerated, but it sounded totally believable to me.

I was desperate to find out more about the school. Why hadn't Kennedy High School reacted more quickly to the concerns raised by pupils when the Forrest–Gemma rumours began? Why hadn't they tried to contact me with more urgency if the concerns were so worrying? I only lived round the corner, after all.

If I was truly a mother who didn't care, who didn't act when they contacted me previously, or who didn't show an interest in the education of my children, why didn't they report their concerns to the social services or the police sooner?

Where was the genuine care any parent should expect from a school? How had this been able to happen right under the school's nose for so long with no one taking any action? Moreover, how had they previously been able to achieve an 'Outstanding' Ofsted rating? Kennedy High School continued to publicly declare that they had 'robust safeguarding policies', but Douglas Sinclair's review had shown that they weren't exactly acting on everything they preached.

There were so many questions swimming around in my head, but I couldn't focus on them right now. I had a family to look after and now that the East Sussex Local Safeguarding Children Board had confirmed that a serious case review was to go ahead, I had to trust that the full truth would be revealed. I would be expressing my views to the panel for my part in the report and eagerly awaited the meeting I would be called to. More than anything, though, I was waiting for this process to finish so that I could get some answers.

CHAPTER 23

FACE TO FACE
WITH FORREST

While the process of adding the charge of sexual activity with a minor was still being argued over at the European Court of Justice, things were moving on with the abduction charge over here.

On Friday, 25 January, Forrest went before the court again, this time for a plea and case management hearing at Lewes Crown Court in front of Judge Mr Justice Singh. At this hearing, he would have to enter a plea of guilty or not guilty rather than just keep silent when asked.

I had never been able to understand why he had not already pleaded guilty at his previous court appearances. There was so much overwhelming evidence of an abduction. No way would he be able to get away with his crime, so what would have been the point of him pleading not guilty?

I couldn't see how he could be anything other than guilty.

The police told me the definition of child abduction is the unauthorised removal of a minor from the custody of the child's natural parents or legally appointed guardians. Had I given Forrest permission to take Gemma to France, he would have had no crime to answer to but I was 100 per cent certain that I had never signed any kind of permission slip and, given Gemma's biological father refused to have his name on her birth certificate, I am the only person who would have been able to sign anything like that to allow her to go.

I had racked my brains trying to work out if there was any way that a permission form could have slipped through without me remembering. Over and over I replayed events in my mind, wondering if maybe this was the key defence that Forrest's legal team would eventually pull out of the bag.

While I had not been in court on the previous occasions when Forrest had been called to enter a plea, I decided to go along to this hearing. By this point, I had become increasingly obsessed with what kind of man he was and so I wanted to see him for myself. At the earlier court sessions, Forrest had appeared via videolink, but DI Neil Ralph told me that he expected him to attend the Lewes Crown Court session in person.

Naturally I was incredibly nervous about seeing him in the flesh. I wasn't intending to go to the court to make a scene or anything, I just wanted to see the creature who had taken my daughter. It would have destroyed Gemma if I'd been unable to control my feelings in court and 'kicked off', as she put it, and behaving in that way would have put me in contempt of court. There was no way that I was going to let that happen.

Out of courtesy, Neil Ralph let Judge Mr Justice Singh know that I was going to be attending court that day. I was legally entitled to be there, but he wanted him to know anyway.

Neil also briefed me about some of the other people who might be in the public gallery for the hearing. With so much publicity about the case, Forrest had attracted a weird fanbase of supporters and very likely some of them would be there for him. Several 'followers' claiming to be in love with Forrest had attended his last court session. They didn't have any connection with him, they were just swept up in the 'romance' of the story.

Gemma wasn't allowed to attend court because she was the victim of the crime, but I promised her that I would get in touch with her as soon as the session had come to an end and tell her all about it.

Before we went into court, Paul, my friend Chloe and I went for a coffee. I was shaking like a leaf. It was such a surreal experience that I would be coming face to face with my daughter's abductor any minute now. It was incredibly frightening.

I then met up with the prosecution barrister, Richard Barton, and he was lovely with me. I know I say that about almost everyone connected to the case, but I really have been so very lucky with the teams of people who have worked on it. Richard took me to one side and reassured me that everything was going to be fine and said that if there was anything that I didn't understand, he would be more than happy to explain any details. I knew we were very lucky to have him on our side, as there seemed to be nothing he didn't know about the law. I had every faith in him that he would do his utmost for us.

There was so much going on. People seemed to be rushing from one office to another and pieces of paper were being handed round as the legal teams got everything in order before the session began.

It was then that Mark Ling dropped the bombshell that he had heard that Forrest was likely to be entering a plea of not guilty. My heart sank to the pit of my stomach. In pleading not guilty, there would have to be a trial and that would mean that Gemma would be forced to give evidence in court.

Completely thrown, I couldn't take in what Mark was saying. There was going to be a trial – and what's more, in all likelihood it would be smack-bang in the middle of Gemma's final GCSE exams. I was told that the Crown Prosecution Service would be calling 14 witnesses at the trial, and I could only guess that these were likely to be police officers, teachers, other pupils, Forrest's wife and, of course, Gemma and myself.

It was only when we got into the court and saw a video screen that we realised that once again Forrest wouldn't be appearing in person. I was disappointed – I had fretted for days and got myself so psyched up that I was going to see him in the flesh. I wanted to have a chance to take in every detail of him – to see what he looked like up close and to try and understand how he had made Gemma fall for him.

The videolink was switched on and the next thing I saw was Forrest coming to take a seat in front of the camera. He seemed to be having a joke with the cameraman. I was so angry that he had the audacity to act like that – this was no laughing matter. He then slumped down in the chair, which made me dislike him even more. His attitude really got under my skin.

As in previous court appearances, the judge asked him to plead guilty or not guilty. The bile rose in my stomach as I heard him speak.

'Not guilty.'

I still didn't believe it. I wanted him to say it again and again, just so I could be sure of his words. After that, the next part of the hearing was all a bit of a blur as I was still trying to get my head around the idea of him pleading not guilty. At one point, I recall that Judge Mr Justice Singh asked Forrest's team if they had prepared their defence statement, and they said that they still had nothing to offer. The judge seemed to be furious and set them a deadline of mid-March to submit the necessary information.

I was totally confused. What kind of game was his team of hotshot lawyers playing? But they just smugly looked on as if biding their time.

It was announced that Forrest would face a two-week trial at Lewes Crown Court from Monday, 10 June. The whole session was over in a matter of minutes.

Standing outside the court afterwards, we tried to take stock of what had just happened. I was trying to make sense of his not guilty plea. Why had he done it? I started to worry about what he would have to say when the trial began. Once again, I began to wonder if perhaps I had actually given permission for Gemma to go away with him. I was certain I hadn't, but I couldn't understand for the life of me why he hadn't pleaded guilty.

I was terrified about the impending trial. It wouldn't just be Gemma in the firing line – I knew that anyone that the Crown Prosecution Service wanted to act as a witness would have to be there, too. That meant me, Forrest's wife, Gemma's schoolfriends and a whole string of other innocent victims.

As we were standing there, I caught the eye of Forrest's solicitor and I felt really intimidated. He gave me a kind of look that seemed to say: 'We're going to win this ...'

CHAPTER 24

GEMMA'S PLEA

I had promised that I would report back to Gemma as soon as I had any news, but I knew that this kind of information couldn't be relayed to her over the phone, so I waited to get home before I told her what had happened.

She burst into tears the moment she heard the word 'trial'. Upset, angry and confused, she was adamant that she wouldn't go to court: 'You can tell them now, I won't be doing anything.'

'But, sweetheart,' I said, 'you have to ...' She ran upstairs to my room and slammed the door.

I knew that she needed space and time to get her head around what was happening so I left her alone. I didn't know what I was meant to do. I rang the police and asked for advice about how I should handle the situation, and they said that I should try not to panic because the trial was still a long way off. For all we knew, Forrest could yet change his plea and the trial might not happen anyway.

After an hour or so, I checked in with Gemma to see if she wanted anything to eat or drink. She was still in a real state and begged me to change what I'd said to the police. If I said I had actually given Forrest permission to take her away, she said, then he wouldn't have a case to answer to.

But that wasn't true. I would never have given Forrest permission to take Gemma out of the country.

She continued to plead with me to change my statement. I have to admit that I did consider it briefly, as I just couldn't face the heartache that the trial would bring. But it would have been a lie and I could have ended up in prison myself. Besides, I wanted justice. We just had to accept the inevitable: there would be a trial and the nightmare would continue.

Lee was concerned that he would be called as a witness, as he had seen Gemma from a distance walking to Louise's house with another friend on the night she had said goodbye to me. None of us knew yet who the Crown Prosecution Service would want to appear at the trial, and I tried to explain the situation as best I could to Lee and Maddie. I was determined to be as open with them as I could, and assured them that I would try to get answers for anything that was worrying them.

My poor mum was devastated when I told her that the case was going to go to trial. At sixty-seven, she was battling with various conditions, including arthritis, sciatica and an irregular heartbeat, and during this time her health really went downhill. Prior to Gemma going missing, the two of them had always had the most wonderful relationship, but it had all fallen apart.

Up until this point, I had spared Mum a lot of the details of the case as I knew she wouldn't have been able to handle it; it wouldn't have been fair to burden her with it. When she would ring up, I would tell her that things were fine to stop her from worrying. Now, though, there was going to be a trial and there was no way we would be able to avoid her finding out what had happened.

We talked about how she used to spoil Gemma with her favourite meals and how unhappy she was that they didn't talk anymore. At one point, she remembered Gemma once telling her that her boyfriend had written a song about her that included the lyrics 'You hit me like heroin'. She remembered remarking, 'That's a bit strong for someone of your age, isn't it?' and the conversation had quickly tailed off after that. Gemma didn't mention him again and Mum had forgotten the conversation had ever taken place. They didn't really have heart to hearts any more after that.

It was such a shame – they used to have such a tight-knit relationship before this. Mum lived with my sister Charlotte and her husband and daughter, and Gemma would often go and stay with them. They had even talked about going on holiday to Disneyland Paris together. Funnily enough, this became significant when the police investigation got underway. Mum and Charlotte's laptops were seized after Gemma went missing as the police knew she would have used them when she stayed over with them and, lo and behold, they found internet searches for Paris on the browser history. We had to explain that they were just planning an innocent family trip to Disneyland Paris, not a secret runaway.

CHAPTER 25

MORE DETAILS REVEALED

B it by bit, the police were piecing together what had happened when Gemma went missing, and we began to get a sense of just how chillingly calculating Forrest had been when he abducted her.

On the day that Gemma had told Louise that she wasn't feeling well and that she was going to go back home, she had instead gone to a shopping centre car park, where Forrest was waiting for her.

Gemma had left her wash bag at Louise's. Apparently, when they went back to pick it up, Forrest was in tears and cried to Louise, 'I'm sorry I'm doing this, but I have to.' It was if he was trying to manipulate Louise into thinking he was making some sort of grand gesture by running away with Gemma and wanted the poor girl to feel sorry for him. I expect he thought the fact that a teacher was trusting her with private information would make her more likely to keep the secret. He was a grown-up, after all, and Louise would have liked the fact he was confiding in her.

The first Gemma knew that they were going to France was when they were in the car on the way to Dover to catch the ferry. It was at this point that she first began to realise the magnitude of what she was doing. She had wanted to run away from home because she knew that she was going to be in trouble for lying about what had been going on with Forrest, but she had never factored in a trip abroad; she had just assumed they would go to Scotland or somewhere up north. She didn't speak to Forrest for the rest of the journey. She was scared, but felt it was too late to go back.

Before the ferry crossing, Forrest got Gemma to send a text to her friend Ben, telling him that they were heading north. Again, I think he thought Ben would be thrilled to be included in their circle of trust, but he also wanted to make sure that he had left a false trail in case Ben later said anything to the police. He had it all sussed out.

He later chucked his phone in the sea and, knowing the police would likely be on their tail, dumped his car soon after driving to Paris – he knew they were in danger of being tracked through the toll roads. From Paris, they then caught a train to Bordeaux.

It was so disturbing to discover how much Forrest had planned before the trip. He even told Gemma that he had researched what his prison sentence could be for taking her. It made me feel sick. In France, the legal age of consent is fifteen – provided, that is, the adult isn't in a position of responsibility, which of course he was.

Forrest wanted to blend in as Gemma's boyfriend rather

than her teacher, to lay low in France until her sixteenth birthday and then resume their relationship back in the UK afterwards. Just because he was in France, though, didn't mean he was invisible.

It transpired that he had created a fake CV using the name Jack Dean and had applied for a job working in a bar in Bordeaux. The manageress of the bar was British and had read about Gemma's case online. She realised who Forrest was and, liaising with police, invited him back for a second interview.

He and Gemma were intercepted by plain-clothed policemen while on their way back to the bar. It was there that Gemma thought she was being kidnapped and so she started screaming and trying to claw free to get away. It wasn't until Detective Inspector Andy Harbour called out to Gemma and started speaking to her in English that she started to calm down.

Alison, the woman who blew the whistle on them in Bordeaux, was interviewed after their discovery. 'They seemed really nice and she seemed normal, no sign of distress, but I don't feel their plan was thought through well enough,' she said. 'We might live in France, but we do follow what happens in our own country. As soon as I logged on to the internet, I recognised their photos.'

CHAPTER 26

NEW HOUSE, NEW START

On Tuesday, 5 February 2013, two letters arrived in the post confirming that Gemma and I would have to attend court for the trial hearing. I decided to hide them – I just couldn't face telling Gemma about them. Already she was in such a state thinking about the trial.

I told Sarah and we agreed that it would be best if I waited until nearer the time to tell her, when we would know for certain if the trial was going to be taking place. We agreed that Gemma didn't need the additional worry and uncertainty.

A week later, another alarming letter arrived. This time it was from Kennedy High School, asking if Gemma would like to take up the offer of their post-sixteen courses after Year 11. I couldn't believe they had the nerve to send me something like this. I thought about sarcastically replying with some suggestions about the kind of courses the school could actually take itself – child safety, for example – but I resisted the temptation and just filed it for the time being.

In the meantime, with so many things happening that were beyond our control, we were getting much closer to finding the kind of house that we needed. I ordered a skip and looked forward to its arrival, knowing I could put all my energies into something positive for a change. It was ironic as I'd been in the process of ordering one on the day that Gemma disappeared, but back then it was an entirely different situation.

It was good to have a big clearout, as I could get rid of all the bad memories and get ready for a fresh start. But just our luck, yet again things didn't go exactly to plan …

On the day that the skip was delivered, Paul suddenly called out from upstairs, 'Is Milly in the kitchen with you?' Milly was our Yorkshire Terrier and I'd had her for 12 years, since she was an eight-week-old puppy. She was given to me by my stepdad on the last day I ever saw him, so she was very special to me. Anyway, on the day the skip arrived, the back gate was left open and Milly escaped. She was a tiny little thing and had squeezed through impossibly small spaces before, but she had always previously come back home.

This time, however, she never did. We searched high and low for her – as did the neighbours who knew and loved her, too – but it was no use, she was gone. With yet another trauma to cope with, I was heartbroken. I didn't feel I could go round the neighbours asking if they'd seen her when only recently I'd been asking if they'd seen my daughter. In the end my next-door neighbour Katrina went round for us, but it was all to no avail: Milly was gone.

Finally, on Saturday, 9 March we moved into our new home.

It ended up happening quite quickly. We knew as soon as we saw the house that it was the perfect place for us. What's more, it was brand new, so there were no unhappy memories that could be attached to it.

Before we signed on the dotted line, I took the children round to see the house and showed Gemma the room that would be hers. I promised her a new bed, new bedroom furniture, new bedding – the whole lot. I wanted her to feel she had her own space again after so many months of sleeping on the sofa. She absolutely loved it. It was so lovely to see her happy again. 'Finally,' I thought, 'we can get things back on track.'

Come the day we moved, we decided that we wouldn't make a big deal about leaving. We agreed that we wouldn't tell the neighbours where we were going as we were concerned someone might inadvertently mention it to the press later. I was sad that I couldn't say goodbye properly to everyone. If I could have picked up all of the neighbours and relocated them to our new street, I would have done – they were such great people.

Excited as I was about moving to a new house, I felt sad, too. I had lived in our old house for 10 years and, apart from the traumatic last nine months or so, I had lots of happy memories of my time there. It was where Lee, Gemma and Maddie had grown up, and it was Alfie and Lilly's first home, so it wasn't all bad there.

The first night in the new house was fabulous. I actually slept that night, rather than just laying there hoping that at some point my body would shut down. Being able to wake up in the morning and knowing that no one knew we were 'that family' was an amazing feeling. Just being able to say good morning to our new neighbours like any other ordinary people was a real joy. I didn't feel the urge to have to introduce myself or explain that all the stuff about me online wasn't true.

It was great to be anonymous and normal again.

CHAPTER 27

WORK-LIFE BALANCE

The following month, April, I went back to work. The company I was working for had been incredibly supportive and allowed me to extend my maternity leave because of the Gemma situation, but I knew that I had to try and start earning money again.

Beforehand, Gavin, my line manager, did everything he could to prepare me for coming back to work and even organised some occupational therapy for me – to assess how my job might need to be adapted because of the change in my circumstances. Previously, I had regularly been required to work extended hours and sometimes had to stay away from home overnight. Clearly, given everything that was going on, I could no longer do this. It was agreed that I would initially work three days a week and we would then review the situation going forward.

My first day back coincided with a big department meeting up in Manchester and I decided that I was going to brave it head-on and attend. Paul was working for the same company at the time and was also going to the meeting, so we arranged for Maddie and Alfie to stay with Max, my ex-husband. Lee, meanwhile, was staying over at his girlfriend's and Paul's mum came over to stay to look after Gemma and Lilly.

So there I was at the meeting, all suited and booted and ready to go. The people there were all so caring and understanding, and the head of department kicked off proceedings by welcoming me back. Everything was kept really light-hearted. I had been with the company for 10 years and had lots of friends whom I had stayed in touch with while I was away, so there was no awkwardness with close colleagues. Of course, some people there didn't know me well and didn't really know what to say to me, but that was fine – I realised it wasn't exactly an everyday situation to be in.

The meeting went well and I was all set to get back to work and looking forward to getting back to my usual routine. Luckily, my job involved working with teams of young people and I was always called by my first name, so my workmates would be unlikely to spot the link between me and Gemma's case. The court order came in really handy in this respect because my name was no longer being used in the press coverage. Obviously the senior management team was aware of it, but those who knew what was happening were very respectful and didn't mention anything.

My job required me to audit stock in stores all over the south of England. It involved quite a lot of travelling, as the company was revamping the stores and implementing a new system. I was working between a number of stores, managing different teams in several areas, and I was looking forward to being able to step out of the chaos at home and be someone else for three days a week.

I knew it would be a real shock to the system to begin with, having to get up at 6.30am and getting the kids dressed, fed and off to nursery and school, but once I was sitting on the train for my commute into work, I would be able to breathe and step out of all of the stresses of Gemma's situation. It was a great feeling to know I was going to be a working mum again.

I took pride in the way I dressed – I think it's important to look professional for work – and it felt good to have to wear dresses and make-up again. I'd lived in loose, comfy clothes after Lilly was born, but now I was back being me. Working in all sorts of different locations meant I would have plenty of time on the train to get my thoughts together, to process what was going on at home and face the challenges ahead.

But my dream of getting life back on an even keel didn't last long.

When I returned from Manchester with Paul, everything seemed fine at home. Paul's mum said that she and Gemma had had a really nice time together with no dramas. Then Gemma took one look at me and snapped. I snapped back: 'Don't talk to me like that!' With that, she said, 'I'm sick to death of this, I'm sick to death of you!', and stormed upstairs.

She then came downstairs with her bags packed, saying she was going to stay with Max. She claimed I wasn't telling her everything and complained that I was siding with the police and the social workers. I knew she was in a very bad place, but I'd always tried so hard to tell her everything I knew about the case. I had given her a list of numbers of

Above left: A close-knit family: Gemma with her older brother and younger sister.

Above right: Mother Davina Williams attends the press conference appeal to find her daughter.   © *Rex Features*

Below: The runaway schoolgirl and Forrest were eventually spotted walking hand in hand on the rue Sainte Catherine in Bordeaux, France. © *Roland Hoskins/Associated News/REX*

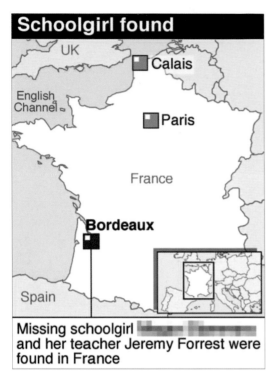

Schoolgirl found

Missing schoolgirl ███████ ████████ and her teacher Jeremy Forrest were found in France

Above left: Graphic revealing the place where the schoolgirl and her teacher were found.

© *PA Graphics/Press Association Images*

Above right: The 15-year-old boards a plane at Bordeaux airport on 29 September 2012.

© *Bob Edme/AP/Press Association Images*

Below: Reunited: Gemma cuddles her baby sister.

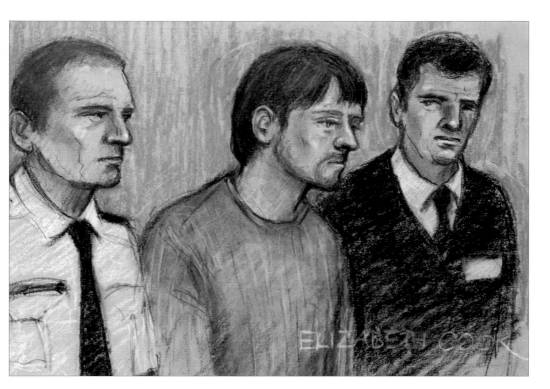

Above: A court artist drawing of Jeremy Forrest appearing at Eastbourne Magistrates Court, where he was remanded in custody charged with abducting a pupil.

© *Elizabeth Cook/PA Archive/Press Association Images*

Below: Lewes Crown Court: the location of Forrest's trial for child abduction.

© *Rex Features*

Forrest arrives at
Lewes Crown Court.
© Gareth Fuller/PA Wire

everyone involved and had told her that they would be only too happy to go through any details with her, but she never once called anyone.

I just wasn't telling her what she wanted to hear – she wanted me to tell her that everything would turn out alright and that she would soon be back with Forrest – and she hated me for it. She knew, too, that I hated the parasites who were trying to befriend her, but as far as she was concerned, they were the only ones on her side. The way she saw it, I was just against her the whole time.

She called Max and he came and picked her up. He shrugged – he knew that I'd tried my hardest to make things work with her, but he wanted to be a good dad for her, too.

When I called Max later that night to check everything was OK, he told me that he thought she just needed some space away from the constant phone calls and appointments with the police, support workers and various other people involved with the case. I could understand that, but I was worried she might run away again. I was also concerned that she had become unhealthily close to that woman in Hertfordshire. After all, that awful woman had been to see Forrest in prison, and I am sure that she would have been only too happy to offer Gemma a place to stay.

For the time being, though, she was staying put at Max's and I was getting regular reports back that things were OK. Max and I have differing views on parenting at times. He wanted to allow Gemma more space, but I was concerned about how she had been affected by everything that had happened over the past few months. I thought she was broken and needed much closer attention. I wouldn't have been surprised in the slightest had she decided to head up to

Hertfordshire on the spur of the moment, or turned up on the doorstep of Forrest's parents.

In the past, when we had previously had typical parent–child disagreements, Gemma and I always stayed in touch by text – the odd word such as 'You OK?' or 'Goodnight', things like that. We both hated falling out with each other and those texts were very important to us both because we knew, underneath it all, that we still loved each other very much. I know it seems odd to some people that we can be not speaking to each other and yet still texting one another, but that's just the way we are. So when the texts from Gemma totally stopped I was heartbroken. She didn't want anything to do with me. I wrote her a long email, telling her how much I loved her, and I continued to send her 'I love you' texts, but I got no reply.

I tried nice texts, loving texts and then, finally, an angry text. The second I sent it I regretted it. I immediately sent an apology text, but heard nothing back.

After a few days, I thought that's it, she's not coming back. I remember sitting watching the ABBA film, *Mamma Mia!*, and hearing the song, 'Slipping Through My Fingers', about a young girl growing up and leaving home. Tears started to stream down my face – I knew my darling Gemma had slipped through my fingers, too.

Every line of that song was so poignant – 'That feeling that I'm losing her forever. I let precious time go by. Then when she's gone, there's that odd melancholy feeling, and a sense of guilt I can't deny. Each time I think I'm close to knowing, she keeps on growing, slipping through my fingers all the time ...'

I had lost her and there was nothing I could do about it.

In desperation, I spoke to Sarah and she said that I should

try writing all of my feelings in a letter to Gemma, so I did, scanning pictures of her when she was a little girl and sharing the memories I had of her. I wanted her to remember how much we'd been through together and I was in floods of tears as I wrote to her. I lost count of how many times I started the letter, but finally I finished it and posted it off to her.

But still I heard nothing back from her.

I didn't know it at the time, of course, but she was to stay at her dad's until after the trial. I missed her so much and blamed myself for driving her away.

CHAPTER 28

LAST-CHANCE SALOON

Although it was pretty much a foregone conclusion that a trial would be taking place, Forrest was given one more chance to make a plea of guilty and avoid the inevitable nightmare for all concerned. If only he would admit to the crime that was so obvious to the rest of us, we could start to put this whole nightmare behind us.

So, on Friday, 17 May, I found myself back in Lewes Crown Court again, this time with my friend Chloe and Sarah, as Paul couldn't get the time off work. On this occasion, Forrest would definitely be there in person – he had no choice in the matter – and so, once again, I psyched myself up to see him face to face.

Forrest's parents and his sister Carrie also attended. His mother Julie's face had the same drained look that I'd seen during the press conference she and her husband Jim had given, back in September. Their daughter appeared to be comforting her and Jim Forrest was deep in conversation with the barrister and solicitor. It seemed that he was the one dealing with all the legal processes.

Sitting right behind us there was a line of reporters. Chloe whispered in my ear: 'Don't react, don't say anything.' I just sat there between Chloe and Sarah, clutching their hands.

When Forrest was brought up into the defendant's box, I couldn't take my eyes off him. I wanted to take in every detail of this bastard who had taken my child's innocence.

He was wearing a badly fitting suit, but he looked relaxed and gave his family a thumbs-up and mouthed the words 'I'm fine'. All I could do was stare and stare at him. If my eyes could have burnt into him, he would have been in flames. At one point, he flicked his eyes over to me for less than a second, but he never looked at me again.

As soon as the proceedings started, his body language changed and he went from being casual – maybe even cocky and relaxed – to much more upright and respectful. He put his hands down by his sides, as if he'd been coached to look as open and trustworthy as possible.

The judge came in and, after all the required legalese had been delivered, asked Forrest to stand up. He asked him how he pleaded: guilty or not guilty?

Once again, those chilling words …

'Not guilty.'

As I sat there, trying my very hardest not to react, I could hear the reporters' pens scratching at their notepads as they scribbled away furiously. I held Sarah and Chloe's hands in a vice-like grip. Every shred of emotion I was feeling went into my fingers. This wasn't happening, was it?

I had promised that I wouldn't make a scene in court. Now I was actually there with him in front of me, it took every cell in my body to stop myself from standing up and screaming, 'You're a bastard! Do you know what you're doing to my daughter?' But with Sarah and Chloe's support, I was able to stay calm, although it took one hell of a lot of effort not to let my emotions fly.

I thought back to the initial statement that I had given to the police when Gemma disappeared. They had asked me if I'd given Forrest permission to take her out of the country and I had told them that no, I most certainly had not.

At the time, they had told me that this was all the evidence they would need to find him guilty of abduction. I also had Gemma's words in my head: that if I could just change my statement then all of this would go away. Except it couldn't just 'go away'. I couldn't just change my statement and I knew in my heart of hearts that, painful as all of this was going to be, it was the right thing to do.

Afterwards, outside the court, chief inspector for child protection Mark Ling, DI Neil Ralph and the prosecution barrister Richard Barton came over to talk to us, and I could see Forrest's family out of the corner of my eye. At one point, I saw his sister making a move to come over to me, but she was held back by her mum. I was unnerved, as I didn't know if she wanted to talk to me or have a go at me – I still wonder now what she would have said to me.

The press wanted me to give them a statement, but I refused. I was too upset to put my feelings into words. I'd been given plenty of opportunities to speak to the press, but I never did – I just couldn't bring myself to do it. I was always worried what would be said about my family and my parenting skills, not to mention the impact it was having on my children.

The crazy thing was, if Forrest had admitted to the crime months ago when he first appeared at Eastbourne Magistrates' Court, he would most likely have been walking free by now. The judge would have taken his swift plea, good behaviour and cooperation into account. Instead the nightmare was about to step up a gear. The trial was set to begin in just over three weeks' time, on Monday, 10 June.

There was no escaping the fact that we faced a trial, and Gemma would have to be involved, whether or not she was happy about it. We had to get her to understand that. As much as she hated the words 'victim' and 'witness', she was both.

Mark Ling visited Gemma at Max's house and explained to her as gently as he could that she was going to be called as a witness. If she refused to attend court, the judge would have no option but to subpoena her. Should she then refuse to follow the subpoena, she would be arrested.

One way or another, she had to go to court. Mark Ling tried to make her understand that it was the Crown Prosecution Service who were bringing the case against Forrest, not her family, and that she had no choice about whether or not she could attend. But no matter what Mark, Max or anyone else said about it, Gemma remained defiant: she wasn't going, and that was that.

The victim support team invited her to go and have a look round the courtroom, so that she wouldn't be so daunted on the actual day that she would have to stand as a witness. They thought that if she was more familiar with the surroundings, it wouldn't seem so scary. They must have asked me a dozen times, and I passed on all their messages via Max but again, there was no way she was going to change her mind.

In the meantime, Gemma had her GCSEs to get through. Although this would normally be one of the most challenging periods in a teenager's life, in a strange way it was helpful because it gave her another focus in life other than the court case. By this point, she had started to go off the rails a bit and was not attending FLESS when she should, but Max and I agreed that it was important for her to attend her exams, and he promised to ensure that she turned up for them.

As had previously been arranged, Gemma went back to Kennedy High School to sit her exams. Unfortunately, the arrangements they made for her were woefully inadequate. It would have been too distracting for her to sit with her old classmates, so instead they stuck her in a room by the reception, hardly the right conditions for sitting an exam. To make matters worse, the laptop they gave her to use didn't work properly and the printer was out of ink. Not surprisingly, after this disastrous start, we decided we had no choice but to make other arrangements and she was very quickly moved to another school to sit the remainder of her exams.

Needless to say, I didn't have very high expectations for Gemma's results. With everything that had been happening, I took it for granted that she wouldn't get any decent grades. Once again, though – and I can say it very happily this time – I was wrong. Gemma did brilliantly. Sadly, of course, at the time I had no idea how the exams were going because she was still refusing to speak to me. I was so grateful for all the support that FLESS had given her, she never would have got through her exams otherwise.

CHAPTER 29

A SIGNIFICANT BIRTHDAY

On Gemma's fifteenth birthday the year before, we had talked about how her sixteenth was going to be extra-special. As a family, we have always made a big thing about 'significant' birthdays – five, thirteen, sixteen, eighteen and so on – so this year was going to be a real treat. Gemma had even been talking about where she would like to go, ruling out where she didn't like before then moving on to her next choice.

All of that, of course, was long before this terrible period when all of our lives had been turned upside down. I hadn't spoken to her since she had left home and moved in with Max, and she wasn't acknowledging my texts, so I had a heavy heart, knowing I wouldn't be part of her birthday that year.

As we got closer to her sixteenth birthday on Sunday, 2 June, I became very quiet and withdrawn. Paul was really lovely and caring with me, saying there would be other years we could celebrate together and reassuring me that this was only a temporary problem in our relationship. But all my efforts to reconnect with her had failed. I was finding it very difficult to come to terms with the fact that she had totally blanked me out of her life.

Max was very understanding about the situation and reassured me that he would make sure that Gemma had a great birthday. He arranged to take her out for a nice meal with the rest of his family and I knew he would make a big fuss over her. In a way, selfishly, that made things worse for me because I wanted to be part of it.

Gemma loves make-up and perfume, so I bought her some nice treats and took Paul's advice to leave a special present for another time when we could properly celebrate as mother and daughter again. Even so, I didn't let up trying to contact her and really hoped that she would get in touch.

Then I heard that she had been hearing stories – I don't know who from – that I didn't want to see her or have any-thing to do with her again. I can only think it was the online parasites trying to drive a further wedge between us. Now I was coming up against brick wall after brick wall and people seemed determined to keep us apart.

On the day of her birthday, I kept hoping that she would come back home but it wasn't to be. Maddie took Gemma the presents we had got her, and about an hour later, I got a text from Gemma. All it said was 'thank you'. It wasn't much, but at least it was something – I was thankful that she had been in touch at all. Paul put his arm round me. 'You've done the right thing,' he said.

Max continued to reassure me that Gemma was OK and that, despite the looming trial, she was still able to enjoy her birthday. I wasn't jealous of him as such, I was just upset that I couldn't be with her, knowing it was another day of my daughter's childhood that Forrest had stolen from me.

The trial date was getting much closer now – it was due to start in a week's time, on Monday, 10 June 2013. Finally, after months of waiting, I would be able to get some answers to why Forrest had been able to destroy our lives.

PART TWO

THE TRIAL

CHAPTER 30

DAY 1:
MONDAY, 10 JUNE

And so, finally, the trial that we had all been dreading began.

I knew that I wouldn't be able to sit in the courtroom until I had taken the stand to give evidence, but I was determined to be nearby throughout the trial. I knew, too, that I couldn't be told anything about what had happened until then either, but it didn't matter to me: I just had to be there.

The original plan was for Paul to come with me every day. Paul and I had taken two weeks' holiday leave and his mum had kindly said she would move in and look after Alfie and Lilly for the duration of the trial. We wanted the situation at home to be as normal as possible for the little ones.

Various friends and family members had asked if they could go along and sit in the public gallery. To be quite honest, I didn't know if it was a good idea or not – I wasn't really functioning properly at the time – but I was very grateful that they wanted to be there for me. I feel incredibly lucky to have had such a great support network while living through this nightmare.

Poor Lilly had a terrible night on the Sunday and woke up with a raging temperature. Added to that, Paul's mum was also feeling poorly, so I was torn between staying at home to look after my youngest daughter or going to court to support my eldest one. After much agonising, Paul and I decided that he would stay at home with Lilly and I would drive myself to court. Mum and Charlotte offered to take me, but I thought the 20-minute drive on my own might help me mentally prepare for the fortnight to come. I drove there in silence, trying to get my head around what was in store.

I got to Lewes, parked in a car park a little way from the court and met up with my friends Chloe, Darcee and Sarah. There was a really solemn atmosphere; we were all so nervous about what lay ahead. Sarah tried to reassure me that there was nothing for me to be anxious about – the first day was really just a formality, she explained, with the jury being sworn in and the prosecution presenting their case and so on – but it didn't take away from the fact that we were all so freaked out by the whole experience. We went for a coffee and tried to keep our spirits up, but the silent moments told the real story.

Lewes Crown Court is at the top of a hill, and when we finished our coffees we walked up the hill, laughing about how steep it was. When we reached the top, we saw that there was a crowd of photographers and reporters waiting outside the court and a number of camera crews had set up pitches across the road, and the nerves took over again. As we took in the scene, we wondered how the hell we were going to get into the building without being mobbed by reporters.

We decided to just march straight up there and through the banks of photographers. As soon as we approached them, that dreaded click-click-click-click-click noise fired off from every direction as they craned to get pictures of anyone who was going into the court. It was so frightening.

Once inside, we were helped through the security checks and directed upstairs into the witness services area, where we met a very nice lady who had been assigned to look after us for the duration of the case. Then chief inspector for child protection Mark Ling and DI Neil Ralph came in to check that I was OK, and reiterated to me that I wouldn't be able to go into the courtroom or be told about any of the proceedings until after I had given my evidence. They looked as nervous as me, but then I suppose it was a big deal for all of us: we all wanted everything to go smoothly.

Next the prosecution barrister, Richard Barton, came to see us and he went through the running order of witnesses. Gemma was due to appear tomorrow, after which it would be my turn, followed by Forrest's wife Emily, Gemma's teachers and other kids from her school. He warned me that the running order would be subject to change, depending on how events unfolded.

There were some smaller witness rooms off to the side of where we were waiting and in the main room there was a small TV screen displaying a list of the cases that were being heard that day. I read through the list and there it was: Court 2, Jeremy Ayre Forrest, 10am.

I couldn't take my eyes off it. There was the name of the man who we first knew as Mr Forrest the teacher, then as Jeremy Forrest the abductor and, finally, as Jeremy Ayre Forrest, the accused.

I was already aware that Forrest called himself Jeremy Ayre when he performed as a musician and had used the name on social media sites like Twitter, but I didn't realise until that moment that Ayre was his middle name. It is hard to describe how I was feeling as I saw those words on the screen. I was trying to reconcile how three words could add up to so much destruction. It was only then that I really began to understand what we were about to go through. I felt physically sick.

An announcement came over the PA system: 'All parties in the case of Jeremy Ayre Forrest, please go to court number two'. Suddenly, it was all happening.

Chloe went into the courtroom with Mum and Charlotte, while Darcee and I settled in the witness area for what was to be an interminable wait. We talked about everything and anything, stupid things to try and make the time go quickly, and chatted with the witness services people. Time seemed to hardly move at all. I kept guiltily thinking about my poor baby Lilly and I felt bad that I wasn't at home looking after her. Truth be told, though, she was probably better off being with Paul that day; my nerves were in tatters.

At around midday, the judge, Michael Lawson, QC, adjourned the session for an hour's lunch break and Chloe popped up to see us. I would be lying if I said I wasn't dying to ask her what had been going on, but I knew how important it was that I wasn't told anything at all about the case. All I was allowed to know was that a jury of eight men and four women had been sworn in and that the judge had made his opening statement.

We met up with Mum and my sister Charlotte and went off in search of somewhere away from all the madness of the court and the photographers and press to have lunch. We found a lovely 1950s-style tearoom called Lewesiana, which is where we subsequently went every single day of the case. It was our safe haven.

In a way, I remember thinking at the time it was strange that we were all so worried about the trial – after all, surely there could be no shadow of a doubt that Forrest was guilty of abduction? Gemma and Forrest had been seen boarding the ferry and I knew for sure that I hadn't given him permission to take my daughter away, so the evidence was cut and dried. Whereas previously I had wondered if I might somehow have given him permission by mistake, I was now in a completely different headspace.

I knew for certain that I hadn't; I knew for certain that Forrest was guilty. And yet, even with that knowledge, what scared me was the unknown. He had kept saying, 'The truth will come out', and I was living on my nerves, wondering what the hell he meant when he said that.

I didn't feel like eating and was fretting about Lilly; I'd been in touch with Paul and my baby wasn't feeling any better. But the thing most heavily playing on my mind was the thought of Gemma having to give evidence the next day. I cannot believe any parent would be happy with their child having to do that; the idea of her facing a barrage of questions was just unbearable. I would have made it all stop right there and then if I could, but I couldn't. It was all out of my hands.

Back at the court for the afternoon session, Darcee and I watched people coming in and out of the witness services rooms. To pass the time, we tried to guess what they might be there for. I knew that I wasn't serving any useful purpose being there, but I wanted to be on hand in case there was anything I could help with. I couldn't bear to be anywhere else.

The afternoon session finished at 4pm and we briefly met up again with Mark Ling and Neil Ralph. They reassured me that the afternoon session had gone exactly as planned and told me that Richard Barton had given the opening statement for the prosecution. I knew the gist of what he would have said; it was the defence statement that was totally unknown territory. Maybe then we would finally find out what Forrest meant when he said, 'The truth will come out.'

Back home afterwards, Lilly looked worse than when I'd left her, so I whisked her off to the GP, who informed me that my baby had tonsillitis. I felt so guilty for not having been there for her.

I had sent a couple of texts to update everyone on what was going on, but obviously I didn't have much to tell. As far as actual facts were concerned, all the press could actually report at this point was that the trial had begun, but I knew that they would be stirring up all kinds of stuff about Gemma having bulimia and self-harm issues over the next few days. But I didn't care. I wasn't going to read any of it, I wasn't interested in anyone else's take on what was going on; for me the important thing was to support my family. However, I wanted Gemma to read every single piece of evidence that was coming out about him so that she could understand what kind of man he was.

Today had been nothing, I knew there was much worse to come.

The next day Gemma would give evidence. We still weren't on speaking terms, but I sent her a text: 'I'll be thinking of you tomorrow. If you need me, I'll be there. I love you'. Once again, though, I didn't hear back from her.

Later that evening, Neil Ralph called to confirm with me where Gemma would be the next morning. She was going to be sitting a maths exam at a nearby school first thing, and the plan was for our family liaison officer Hannah and Max to meet her there afterwards and bring her to court. There was still no guarantee that she would go willingly, but I had to trust her to do the right thing.

CHAPTER 31

DAY 2:
TUESDAY, 11 JUNE

After a terrible night's sleep, I got up extra-early. It was Lilly's first birthday and we made a big fuss of her with lots of presents. I had hoped to throw a party for her, but I cancelled it once the trial was confirmed. I know she didn't have a clue what was going on and we could have actually celebrated her birthday any day of the year, but it was a big deal for Paul and me. We had planned to have a bouncy castle in the garden and had been looking forward to everyone having a fun day.

Instead, there she was, feeling so poorly and looking sorrowfully at her presents. I wished I could have split myself in two that day. I left the house feeling full of guilt and sad that there was another moment in my children's life that I would never get back again.

Driving to Lewes, I was a trembling wreck. As I approached

the town, a news report came on the radio – 'Today, the schoolgirl, who we cannot name for legal reasons, is due to give evidence in court in the trial which …' – which only made me feel worse. I immediately switched it off. It felt almost too real to hear it being talked about so publicly. I kept saying to myself over and over again: 'Gemma, sweetheart, please come to court, please come to court …'

I felt sick with worry about how she must be thinking. How on earth was she meant to get through her exam, knowing she would have to go straight to court once she had finished? She had been adamant that she wasn't going to go, but she must have known in her heart that there was no getting away from it. I was scared that she would walk out of the exam, see Max and Hannah waiting for her and try to run away.

I arrived at the car park in Lewes and met up with Chloe, Darcee and Sarah, and they each gave me a reassuring hug. We didn't need to say anything, we all knew that day was going to be a totally different ball game to the previous one.

After a coffee, the walk up the hill and the barrage of the press, we were taken upstairs to the witness services area. This time, though, instead of being taken into the main room, we were led to a side room.

Mark Ling came to see me to check if I was OK and informed me that Gemma had been brought to court and was now sitting in a room two doors up from us. He explained that she would be appearing via a videolink from the witness room, rather than being in the courtroom in person. A court usher would be sitting with her throughout.

It was heartbreaking knowing that she was so close by and not being allowed to go in and see her. If I could have run in and whisked her away, I wouldn't have hesitated; I was so scared for her. All I could think about was what Forrest was putting her through.

I asked the woman who was looking after us in witness services to let Gemma know that I was only two doors away and was there for her if she needed me at all. Everyone knew that she wasn't speaking to me. Max was waiting with her until the session started, but Mark Ling and Neil Ralph reassured me that she was fine.

No matter what anyone said to me, I was feeling like a nervous wreck, and even worse when I heard the dreaded PA announcement. 'All parties in the case of Jeremy Ayre Forrest, please go to court number two'. I could virtually see my heart beating.

With Chloe back downstairs, sitting in the public gallery, Darcee and I got ready for more clock-watching and thumb twiddling. I'd been told that the day would begin with the defence opening statement, after which Gemma would appear via videolink.

After about an hour, Chloe came back to see us. The session had been delayed, as Judge Michael Lawson, QC wanted to speak to Gemma before the cameras were switched on for her to appear via videolink. It gave me great comfort to know how well she was being looked after.

What Chloe told me next came as a surprise. Gemma had asked for the courtroom to be cleared, as she didn't want Mum, Charlotte or Chloe to be there. She seemed to be fine about other people being in the public gallery – including Forrest's parents – and I wondered if it might have been because she didn't want her nan to hear intimate details of her relationship with Forrest.

I didn't have a clue how Gemma would have known that she could request to have the courtroom cleared. Mum was really upset about it. To her, it underlined how badly their relationship had fallen apart. It was so sad; the two of them used to be so close. Chloe tried to reassure Mum that it was probably just because she was embarrassed about the whole thing, but she was heartbroken.

Gemma didn't know Darcee well, and so we decided that she would sit in the public gallery for the afternoon session and keep taking notes for me to read after I had given my evidence. Chloe would wait with me outside the courtroom, while Mum and Charlotte went home.

Whether she liked it or not, Gemma couldn't ask for Sarah, our family social worker, to leave the courtroom. She had initially cooperated with Sarah, but their relationship had deteriorated when she refused to condone her relationship with Forrest or accept it as the great love story that Gemma believed it to be.

Sarah had spent so much time with our family and had seen firsthand how much it had emotionally devastated us. She constantly reassured me that I was doing the right thing and told me that she understood how I felt. Gemma had been molested by a sex offender, and I was struggling to accept it. Even writing those words now makes me feel like the worst mother in the world.

While Sarah had become a lifeline for me, Gemma believed that she was on 'the other side' and wasn't looking out for her at all. Despite everything, though, Sarah and her team never once stopped providing support to Gemma.

Back at court in the afternoon, I saw Forrest's mum and sister waiting to go in the courtroom. His mother and I looked at each other and we shared a kind of half-smile – it was a look that said, 'I know what you are going through'.

I knew that she was suffering as much anxiety and stress as I was. Whatever he had done, Jeremy Forrest was still the son she had given birth to. Obviously, it wasn't like we were about to introduce ourselves and bond over the situation we were in, it was just an unspoken look that said we shared so much.

Darcee went into the courtroom in the afternoon while Chloe and I waited outside.

Later than usual, as there had been a number of breaks while the judge spoke to Gemma, the court session ended for the day. Again, I understood that I couldn't know the exact details of what was going on, but Darcee told us the format of the afternoon. The court had been shown video footage of the long interview Gemma had given at the police house in Hailsham on Wednesday, 3 October, a week after her return from France. Meanwhile, in a corner of the screen, Gemma's live reaction from the nearby witness room was shown.

I was confident that I knew exactly what had been discussed during that interview, so that was one less thing for me to worry about. Gemma had confided in me about what she had talked about with the police, so for once I didn't have that desperate need to know what was going on.

Later I learned that the court was told how the relationship between Gemma and Forrest had started – how she had started following Forrest on Twitter before she went on the half-term school trip to Los Angeles in February 2012, how he had covered for her so that she wouldn't get punished for swimming in the hotel pool without permission, and how she had held hands with him on the flight home.

The court also heard how she had asked a friend to get his

mobile number and they had begun texting one another, how they had kissed each other for the first time in a classroom, and how things got more serious after that. Forrest had apparently sent her a text message which read: 'We can wait until you are 16, but I really want to have intimacy in our relationship'.

Darcee was visibly upset about what she had heard. She has children and grandchildren of her own, so I knew that she would have put herself in my shoes as she listened to the evidence.

Of course, at the time she couldn't tell me what had happened, or how Gemma had been reacting as she was watching the video footage of the interviews, but I was later to find out that Gemma had been really upset.

Totally drained, I went back home and joined Paul and the family. Even though I hadn't actually even been in the courtroom, I felt emotionally exhausted. I took a coffee out to the garden and sat on the swing seat. The next thing I knew, I woke up in a daze and it was 8pm. I had only gone out to clear my mind for five minutes, but I had obviously needed longer to process everything that was happening.

CHAPTER 32

DAY 3: WEDNESDAY, 12 JUNE

Come the next morning, Lilly was still feeling poorly and Paul's mum wasn't yet 100 per cent, so once again we agreed that Paul would stay at home.

I had begun to dread that long, slow walk up the hill from the car park – it was like the green mile. I knew the reporters and photographers would be waiting for me when I reached the top. Having spent five minutes composing myself, I walked towards the court with a grim determination and followed Forrest's family, who had arrived just before me.

Gemma was going to be in court again that morning while further video footage from her police interview was shown. Even though she wasn't going to have to speak while she was there, she still had to attend and be sworn in as any other official witness would be. Meanwhile, Darcee was again in the public gallery, taking notes so that she could tell me what had happened once I had given my evidence.

Chloe and I went back upstairs to the witness services area, but we were starting to feel claustrophobic waiting for the hours to tick by and decided to go for a coffee outside halfway through the morning. We went for a little walk and went window-shopping, and chatted about work, holidays, anything to try and take our minds off the time. Mostly, though, we were just clockwatching, waiting for the morning session to end. Every two minutes, one of us would turn to the other and say, 'What time is it now?'

Lunchtime came round and Mark Ling told me that Gemma would be cross-examined that afternoon and had asked to sit in the courtroom for the session. Upstairs in the witness room, she would have only been able to see Judge Michael Lawson, QC and the prosecution and defence teams on the videolink, and I knew she would have been desperate to see Forrest. She hadn't seen him since September, so I was sure that this was the reason she wanted to be in court.

Normally, if a minor is appearing in court, they give evidence from behind a screen, so it was highly unlikely Gemma would see Forrest while she was giving evidence, but I suppose she would have felt that just being in the same room as him was better than nothing.

We went to the tearoom to take stock of the situation. I don't know if the manager had put two and two together and realised that we had been in court that morning, but he said something along the lines of 'Tough morning?' and showed us to 'our' table in the back of the café. It was quite comforting to go back there every day. He even seemed to have the table ready for us as the days went on.

Instead of spending the afternoon in the witness services area, Chloe and I decided to sit in the corridor – I wanted to be closer to where everything was happening rather than being tucked away upstairs, out of the way. When the doors of the courtroom were open and everyone filed in, I could only really see where the judge would be sitting, but Chloe had described the layout of the court to me the day before. She had also told me that Forrest had been wearing a grey suit and a lilac shirt, and that he was clean-shaven with a closely cropped haircut. He seemed to be taking the whole thing more seriously now.

A little while later, after the doors to the courtroom had been closed, I glimpsed through the glass panels. Instead of being behind a screen, I could see that Gemma had been positioned next to Judge Michael Lawson, QC. She looked so small in comparison, so childlike, but I could tell from her body language that she was trying to look assertive and confident. I think she was hoping to come over as maturely as possible in order to show that she could handle an adult relationship with Forrest.

I suppose I could have lingered at my vantage point to watch how things played out with Gemma in court, but I was mindful about not knowing anything before my turn in the witness box. Besides, it was too upsetting to see Gemma having to give evidence in court. With the videolink, at least I knew she was protected in a secure room, but here everyone's eyes would be burning into her: she was so vulnerable.

Chloe and I tried to fill the hours. When we saw a couple of men outside another courtroom we tried to work out why they were there. We were desperate to find ways to make the time go faster.

While we were sitting there in the corridor, a court reporter came out and made a phone call to his office, describing in graphic detail the evidence that was coming out. 'And their first kiss was in the classroom ...'

Chloe was furious. She marched straight over to him and asked him to show a bit of respect, as Gemma's mum was sitting right there. He apologised and scurried off outside to continue his call.

I obviously looked very different from when I did the press conference, back when Gemma first went missing. I have always taken pride in the way that I look, whereas I looked like an absolute wreck when I appeared at the press conference.

To be fair, I knew that the reporter was only doing his job but it was still a shock to hear someone talking about my daughter like that, rattling off details about Gemma's life like it was some sort of shopping list. It was sickening to hear her being treated like a bit of tabloid fodder and it was going to be hard to stomach reading lurid details of what Forrest did to her.

At 4pm, the court doors opened and everyone spilled out. Once again, Gemma left without saying a word to me.

The moment I saw Darcee, I could tell something significant had happened during the afternoon session. It wasn't just Darcee. I could see the looks of hurt and concern on the faces of other people who had been in the courtroom.

Suddenly, I felt very cold.

Mark Ling and Neil Ralph came up to speak to me as Darcee took Chloe to one side. I could see them whispering to each other and looking concerned. Sarah came over and said: 'You should be very proud of your daughter. She was very articulate and she did really well in there.' Sarah has always said that Gemma was a really lovely, well-grounded child, but the last thing she said to me sounded a bit strange: 'You need to remember the situation she was in.'

I didn't know it at the time, but the evidence that Gemma had been giving that afternoon wasn't tallying with what she had said at her interview in the police house.

Darcee and Chloe came over to give me a hug and reassured me that I shouldn't worry and that it would soon be my turn to give evidence. I stood there looking at them for answers, but I knew I couldn't ask for any more information. What the hell had Gemma been saying in there?

I could sense that something wasn't quite right, but I understood why there was no way that I could be allowed to know what had been said in the courtroom that afternoon. There were restrictions on what the press could report while the trial was taking place, and I was determined to play everything absolutely by the book so that we could get the best outcome possible. I had to stay strong and have faith in everyone to do their jobs. Of course, I would never be able to stop worrying about it, but at least I knew we had a brilliant team on our side.

Just before we all left to go home, Richard Barton told me that I wouldn't be giving evidence after Gemma after all. He had decided to call the teachers at Kennedy High School first as he thought it would be better for the jury to hear what they had to say before getting me on the stand.

I was gutted – I had so wanted to hear them explain how this horrific thing had happened to my daughter. As far as I was concerned, the teachers held the key to this whole horrendous ordeal and the fact that I was going to have to wait even longer to hear their evidence was yet another endurance test.

Richard Barton knew that I really wanted to hear what the teachers had to say, but he felt it was important for the jury to listen to their testimony before mine. I was so disappointed. It goes without saying that I wanted what was best, but I had so wanted to be there to hear them when they started spouting their excuses.

To make matters worse, I was told there would be no court session the next day as Judge Michael Lawson, QC had to attend a retirement lunch, so there was going to be even more of a delay.

Richard Barton also knew that I was keen to give my evidence before Forrest's wife Emily and he confirmed that she would be taking to the stand after me, something I was really relieved about. Firstly, I really wanted to see her in the flesh. I had heard that there was a close resemblance to Gemma and, while I had seen pictures of her in the paper, you can never really tell until you have seen someone for real. More than that, though, I knew that she would be truly honest about what Forrest was like. She knew him better than anyone and I hoped that the expression on her face would tell the true story.

CHAPTER 33

DAY 4:
THURSDAY, 13 JUNE

I was frustrated that we had a court-free day ahead, especially when I'd been so psyched up about giving evidence. As far as I was concerned, the sooner we could get this whole thing over with, the sooner we could get back to living our normal lives. The trial had only been going on for three days, but already it felt like it was dragging on. How were we going to get through it, if it just went on and on?

Although frustrating, I carried on with the day, getting back to my routine of looking after the kids and doing the housework. Alfie went off to school in the morning as usual and I caught up with the washing and housework. It was good to be able to switch off from court and pretend things were normal, if only for a day.

CHAPTER 34

DAY 5: FRIDAY, 14 JUNE

With Lilly feeling a lot better and Paul's mum now well enough to look after her, Paul was able to come to court with me on the Friday. While I'd been grateful for the quiet headspace I'd had during my solo car journeys to Lewes, it was only when I had Paul by my side in the car that I realised how much I needed him with me.

He was relieved to be with me, too. It wasn't just that he felt bad about not being there to support me during the first three days of the trial, but he also felt guilty about what had happened with Gemma and Forrest. He blamed himself for having provided half the money to pay for the school trip to Los Angeles, when Forrest first clawed his way into Gemma's life.

During the drive to Lewes we talked about the morning of that fateful school trip, when I had dropped Gemma off at the coach. I had made her introduce me to the teacher who was supervising her group, and I said to her: 'This is my little girl and I'm trusting you to look after her.' Gemma had cringed with embarrassment at the time as if I was being over-protective, but her teacher clearly didn't do her job.

Like me, Paul felt so much guilt about what had happened. He has never tried to be Gemma's father, but he has always been there for her and they have a good relationship. What had happened to her with Forrest had really taken its toll on him, too.

When we arrived at the court, I checked in with the witness services team to say that I was around, but that I would be downstairs. While there I saw two girls from Gemma's school there to give evidence and I felt really bad for them. It was so sad that they had to go through all this, especially as it was right in the middle of their GCSEs.

I managed a quick hello, but I didn't want to stick around; I knew that I had to keep my distance. To be honest, I don't really know what I would have said to them and their mums anyway, apart from apologising. Nobody wants to see their children put through the trauma of giving evidence in court.

Paul and I decided to go for a walk around Lewes – we probably walked back and forth up Lewes High Street a hundred times that day! But we couldn't think straight and wandered from shop to shop, looking at things but not really seeing them, our minds whirring with thoughts of what was happening in court. We would buy yet more cups of coffee and watch them go cold in front of us – we didn't have the focus to drink, talk or make any decisions, we just drifted.

At about 3pm we went back to the courthouse and waited close to the courtroom for the session to end. Mum and

Charlotte had been back in court that day, as Gemma had completed her evidence and it was now the teachers' turn to be questioned.

I was eager to see the expressions on everyone's faces when the doors opened. As soon as I saw them, I could sense something significant had happened again.

Mum could see that I really wanted to know what had been said. Charlotte quickly turned to her: 'You can't tell her anything!' Charlotte was right, I would find out soon enough. I didn't want to put Mum and Charlotte in a difficult position and so we quickly changed the subject.

It was the same with Darcee and Chloe: they both stood firm. Chloe said, 'You know we can't tell you anything, but we don't want you to worry. Trust us, it's going to be OK.'

One thing made me feel a lot more positive about the situation, though. It was when Chloe turned to me and said: 'I can't wait for you to have your say.'

Whatever the teachers had been claiming had gone on, I knew the truth.

CHAPTER 35

THE WEEKEND: SATURDAY, 15 JUNE AND SUNDAY, 16 JUNE

After a very quiet night on the Friday, an unbelievably long weekend stretched ahead of me. Paul's father had come to stay with us and it was Max's weekend to have Alfie staying with him, so there would be just the five of us, including the newly one-year-old Lilly, who was now bouncing around again almost like her old self.

We decided that we would try to do some nice things as a family, but we were all feeling pretty emotionally drained by the events of the week before. Paul went out and bought all the newspapers, but we just filed them away for later as I was under strict instructions not to read them. It wasn't a problem – we wanted to put the court case on hold for a while and try to act like a normal family.

To be honest, though, there was too much on my mind.

We would put the TV on and start to watch something, but I would just drift off. I couldn't concentrate on anything.

I texted Max to check that everything was OK with Gemma and he replied, saying she was fine. I wondered whether he was just saying that to put my mind at rest, but he told me she was spending some time with friends and that she had been OK.

I had been finding the whole legal process mentally draining and harrowing. I was a whirlpool of emotions. My brain was like a mad pinball machine pinging around fragments of conversations, images of the courtroom and ideas about how it all could play out.

I was like a zombie. I kept falling asleep in random places and would then wake up with a shock and start fretting all over again; I was a mess.

Paul felt absolutely useless, but just a reassuring hug from him meant so much to me. He kept saying, 'I'm so proud of you.' I didn't feel like I'd done anything to be proud of. Again, I was just doing what I thought was right.

CHAPTER 36

DAY 6:
MONDAY, 17 JUNE

It was time for Louise and Ben to testify in court. I wasn't in as much of a state as I had been when Gemma was in the witness box, but I still felt so sad that they had to be there. They were lovely young people and had both been wonderful friends to Gemma. It was such a shame that their special friendship had been destroyed by this whole awful Forrest affair.

Gemma, Louise and Ben had tried to continue their friendship after Gemma got back from France, but there was too much water under the bridge. Louise and Ben had been manipulated into thinking that Forrest had genuine feelings for Gemma, but over time they came to realise that it wasn't all hearts and flowers after all.

They were both very loyal to Gemma and had done everything they could to support her, but they would have said things that she didn't want to hear. Naturally, Gemma would have been upset about this, but the fact that Louise and Ben kept quiet about what had been going on for so long proved what wonderful friends they had been. Like Gemma, I think they were in love with the idea of being in love. They were kind-hearted, good-natured kids from good homes who got swept up in the romance of it all. It just showed how well Forrest had seduced them as well as my daughter.

It was with a heavy heart that Paul and I set off for court again that Monday morning. As usual, we parked in the car park at the bottom of the hill and met the others in the team for a quick coffee before making our way to the courthouse and battling through the ranks of reporters outside. I remember noticing Forrest's dad was outside, talking to the press. I had seen him doing this before; it seemed to me he was almost the 'spokesperson' for the family. Meanwhile, his poor wife just looked lost – she looked how I felt.

Paul and I went to the coffee bar in the courthouse. We no longer felt like we had to keep ourselves hidden away in the witness services area. Forrest's family were there, too, but we all knew our boundaries.

Soon after the morning session began, Paul and I went for a walk in Lewes to buy some gifts for the kids. As he and I wandered around, we started to try and second-guess the kind of questions I would be asked when it was my turn to take my place in the witness box the next day.

I was really panicking about remembering the dates that everything happened. I've always been rubbish at timeframes – I expect I have probably made one or two errors while writing this book, although I can assure you that I have tried my very hardest to get it right!

Mark Ling had reassured me that I would be able to read the

statement that I had given to the police when Gemma first went missing in September, so I knew I would always have that to fall back on. But I also knew that I was going to have to answer questions about Gemma's health – in particular, the fact that the school thought she had bulimia and was self-harming.

I knew all the facts, of course, and I was confident about remembering all the details, it was the dates to go with them that I was worried about. Also, I was concerned that I would lose focus and start waffling under pressure, going off the point of what I had been asked. I really wanted to be crystal clear about what happened.

Paul and I recalled the days leading up to Gemma running away – the call from Miss Shackleton on the day that Lilly was born, the day the police came round, asking about the incriminating pictures on Gemma's phone and so on – when it suddenly struck us that we were doing all this preparation work without really knowing what we were preparing for.

I honestly had no idea what I was going to be asked. All that Richard Barton had said to me was: 'You know what happened, you just have to answer the questions.' He was right, of course; it wasn't as if I had to research the case. His reassuring words really boosted my confidence.

At 4pm, everyone filed out of court. Unlike other days, people seemed to be looking less angst-ridden about what they had heard. I could only guess what Louise and Ben had said, but I found it reassuring to see people's demeanour as they left the courtroom.

Back home that evening, I tried to relax as much as possible, but my mind kept drifting off as I thought about what lay ahead. Even so, I had the kids' dinner to make, lunches for the following day and the usual chores to be getting on with.

Friends had asked me whether I had planned my outfit for the following day – one of them joked that I should dress as a nun to show that I wasn't the shambolic mess that I was being portrayed as on social media – but I didn't give it a lot of thought. The important thing was to try and get a good night's sleep before my big day ahead.

CHAPTER 37

DAY 7: TUESDAY, 18 JUNE

I woke up feeling light-headed. I was so tired, I couldn't think straight and I was more nervous than I'd ever been – worse than before any job interview, driving test or anything. I didn't know exactly what time I would be called to the witness stand, I just knew that it would be at some point that day.

I was terrified.

As we approached the court later that morning, the TV crews were filming me much more closely than usual and the reporters were pushing microphones into my face, asking for comments.

I found it really unsettling. We had been around and about the court for the past week, but now all of a sudden we were the focus of all the press activity. I felt hot and cold, and started to panic. If anyone thinks that I was enjoying all the attention, I can assure you that I did not; the whole thing made me feel sick.

Once inside the court, I said my goodbyes to the friends and family who were heading to the public gallery, and Paul came up to the witness services area with me. As promised, I was given a copy of my initial police statement to read out. I tried to focus on the words, but I just couldn't concentrate on them. I would take a deep breath and start reading again, but I couldn't take anything in. In the end, I just gave up. The woman from witness services said, 'Are you sure you have refreshed your mind enough?' But it was no good, it just wasn't happening.

When the call came for all parties to head to the courtroom for the session to begin, Paul gave me a kiss and wished me luck. I felt so alone when he walked out of the room and started shaking like a leaf. I couldn't control myself. My knees were knocking, my hands were shaking and it felt as if my face was flinching involuntarily. I was worried I wouldn't be able to hold everything together.

The next thing I knew, Mark Ling was by my side. 'Is everything alright? I thought I'd come up and get you.'

It was such a thoughtful thing to do. Before I knew it, I was walking into the courtroom to be met by a sea of faces in front of me. To my left, I saw Paul and around ten other members of my family and friends. They all looked really concerned for me, and my poor Paul started welling up. I knew if any of them had been able to take my place, they would have done so.

As I walked into the courtroom, I looked at the jury, the 12 people who would be deciding the fate of Jeremy Forrest. I couldn't believe how close I was to the reporters who were covering the case and already I could hear their pens scratching away at their notebooks.

When I came in, Judge Michael Lawson, QC gave me a

nice smile, which was lovely of him, but I was still a nervous wreck. He asked me if I would like to sit down.

'Am I allowed?' I asked. I know it sounds a bit daft now, but I was incredibly intimidated by the whole situation.

As my eyes flashed around the room, I took in Forrest, his parents and their defence team before settling my focus on Richard Barton and the judge. I felt as if I had to anchor my eyes to Richard. Otherwise, I thought, my head would wobble around, looking about the room. It was as if I had tunnel vision and could only see who was speaking to me.

I took a deep breath and took my oath on the Bible. I know I said earlier that I am not remotely religious, but swearing on the Bible was very important to me. I promised that I would tell nothing but the truth, and I meant it.

Richard Barton began with the formalities, asking me my name and address, which threw me a bit to be honest, as I had hoped to keep our new address secret from the press. I replied really quickly in the vain hope that the reporters might not catch what I said. For half a second, I thought about saying somewhere different, but I knew that I couldn't.

The next few questions were very straightforward and basically followed what I had said on my statement to the police, back in September. Did I know Jeremy Forrest? Had I had any dealings with him in the past? Was I aware that he was having a relationship with my daughter?

Richard repeated to the jury how Forrest had referred to Gemma as 'a bit of a pain' when he had phoned me and accused her of spreading rumours about the two of them. It seemed clear to me that he wanted the jury to have heard the line about Forrest saying to me that the relationship could ruin his career.

Step by step, he went through all of the events leading up to Gemma's disappearance. I was able to give clear answers with no waffling or forgetting dates. Despite my nerves I found it all extremely easy. After all, the memories he was asking me to recall are those that will stay with me for the rest of my life, whether I like it or not.

Richard picked up on the fact that Forrest had been crying when he was speaking to me on the phone and how I had felt like I was almost counselling him at the time, reassuring him that I would sort the problem out. He asked me how I felt about receiving a call like that and I told him that I was absolutely mortified, how I had always tried to bring up my children to have the utmost respect for teachers, and how embarrassed I was that Gemma had put him in this situation.

I'm not sure how I came across. I don't know if my voice was particularly loud or feeble, but I felt confident in the answers that I was giving. Richard repeated certain key lines for the benefit of the jury. He wanted to make sure he got a clear message to them and that they understood the type of character that Forrest was. We all knew exactly what the true story was, but he needed to make sure that the 12 members of the jury would have no doubt about it either.

Throughout his questioning, I didn't look at the jury. I was just concentrating on making sure I gave my answers as clearly, accurately and succinctly as possible. After around half an hour, Richard concluded my evidence by asking me one final question.

'Did you give permission for Jeremy Forrest to take your daughter to France?'

'No, I did not,' I replied.

I knew this was the killer question, the one that would

surely find Forrest guilty. It was the one response that I wanted everyone to hear as clearly as I could possibly make it.

Richard then said: 'No more questions, your honour.'

It was now time for Forrest's defence barrister, Ronald Jaffa, to stand and start asking me questions. I had seen him going in and out of Lewes Crown Court, and before that at the pre-trial hearings, so I knew what he was like.

As soon as he started questioning me, I felt as if I was under attack.

'I put it to you that your daughter has bulimia.'

'No, she has not.'

'I put it to you that your daughter is self-harming.'

'No, she isn't.'

Where did this line of questioning come from? He was obviously trying to get a rise out of me, but it was going to take a hell of a lot more than that to make me angry.

'I put it to you that your daughter had to leave the country for fear of her life.'

So this was to be Forrest's team's line of defence! They were going to try and make out that the reason he had taken my daughter to France was because he was worried about what would have happened to her otherwise. It was almost as if he was suggesting that I would have killed Gemma, had she stuck around. I was furious.

'No way, that's not true!' I turned to the jury and again said very firmly, 'That is not true.'

It was so quiet in that courtroom, you could honestly have heard a pin drop. I couldn't believe that the defence team's strategy was to blame me, to make out that Gemma had no support at home and couldn't come and tell me how she was feeling.

The judge interrupted proceedings and asked me directly what my relationship with Gemma was like. I told him that it was just a normal mother–teenage daughter relationship. I said that I was fully aware of her pre-existing health problems – I had talked about these in my statement, which the jury had a copy of, so I wasn't holding any information back. I knew she was under pressure because of all of her exams, but we had a normal relationship. Everything had been absolutely fine between the two of us.

I could sense that Ronald Jaffa was seething. His hoped-for trump card had totally fallen flat. Once more, he said: 'I put it to you again that your daughter left this country for fear of her life.' He paused, before quickly adding: 'And she has bulimia!'

And with that, he sat back down like a petulant child. I almost felt like laughing. I had heard that he had previously won some important cases and was really good at his job, but I was thinking, 'Seriously, is that the best you can do?' I almost wanted him to get off his chair and ask me more questions; I couldn't believe that was it.

When the judge then turned to me and said, 'You are now dismissed', it felt like a bit of an anti-climax. The jurors had been provided with an information pack, which included reports from doctors, social workers and the police, showing that Gemma wasn't in fear of her life in any way, and that she wasn't bulimic or self-harming.

Like every mother with a daughter of a certain age, I paid close attention to Gemma's eating habits. At one time I had six pairs of eyes watching her, as close friends and family knew that the school had suggested she had a problem. In fact she was a normal, healthy girl with none of the telltale signs of an eating disorder.

Back outside the court, I met up with family and friends for a group hug. They all said I had done really well and I described how frustrated I'd been about the defence team's line of questioning.

Now, finally, I could be told about what had been going on in the courtroom before that day, and I could begin to understand why my friends and family had been reacting the way they had. Needless to say, Chloe and Darcee couldn't tell me everything that had been said in the space of a lunch break, but they were able to summarise the key information. More than anything, I was desperate to know how Gemma had been in court. What was it that she said that had so upset my family?

I discovered that the responses that Gemma gave when she was cross-examined varied dramatically from the evidence she had given to the police during her interview in Hailsham the previous October. She had changed her evidence to make out that she herself had come up with the idea of going to France and that Forrest was not to blame. She had also told the court that she and I did not get on and that I had not supported her.

Upsetting as it was for me to hear this, I knew it wasn't really Gemma talking. I was hurt, but I had to rationalise her state of mind. She had only just turned sixteen. I didn't want to disregard what she had said, but I didn't feel they were her own words. It was almost as if someone had told her what to say.

Apparently, while Gemma was giving her evidence, she and Forrest often smiled at each other and exchanged glances. I wasn't surprised to hear that; I had suspected all along that was the reason why she wanted to appear in court.

Through my own research into child abuse, I learned that

victims often claim it is their fault that the abuse happened in the first place. That is exactly the behaviour that Gemma displayed in court when she claimed that it had been her idea to start a relationship, rather than Forrest's, and that he had repeatedly urged her not to run away.

What she was saying fuelled some people's opinions that it was just a love story and that the two of them should be together. But if people had actually listened to all of the evidence, it was clear that this wasn't an innocent flirtation. Her words were a textbook response from a victim of child abuse.

I also heard that the teachers had claimed that Miss Shackleton had called me seven times about Gemma and left seven messages. Even though I had just given birth to Lilly, there was no way that I would have ignored seven messages – the one time she left I message I called her back. They were clearly just trying to shift the blame on to me. In any case, if the school really was so concerned that there was an issue to be dealt with, they should have contacted social services – or called me a hundred times, if necessary.

Apparently, the court heard that other teachers and senior members of staff at the school had warned Forrest to stay away from Gemma on several occasions, but he had ignored their instructions. They were painting a very bleak picture of what had gone on at Kennedy High School. Whatever was to happen with Forrest, at least I knew that there was going to be a serious case review, and all the school's shortcomings would eventually be revealed.

Back in the courtroom at 2pm, I took my seat in the public gallery. The next person due to give evidence was Forrest's wife, Emily.

I couldn't believe how close I was to Forrest. I couldn't take my eyes off him and could feel the jury and the press all looking at me, staring at him. But I didn't care what kind of emotions my face showed – I wasn't there to put on a show or impress anyone with my self-restraint either, I just wanted answers.

The usher brought Emily Forrest up to the witness box and, I kid you not, I thought she was a child – she was so small and delicate. I knew she was a year older than Forrest, but she looked like she was the same age as Gemma. She was very pretty and dainty, and really well-spoken, but her voice was childlike. It was really strange.

She took the stand and the prosecution began by asking her about her relationship with Forrest and the events leading up to when he and Gemma went off to France. There was little in her answers that I didn't already know, apart from the news that she and Forrest had been out for dinner together on the Wednesday night before he and Gemma disappeared. She revealed that he had mentioned that he would like them to have a child together and that she had thought it was strange at the time, considering the problems they had been having in their relationship. Back home afterwards, she said that he had 'tucked me up in bed, kissed me on my forehead and said he loved me'.

That's the same night-time pattern I have with my children. I tuck them up, kiss them on their foreheads and tell them I love them. Now I was hearing it was what he did with his wife! It was all so disturbing to listen to, all I could feel was pity.

The court went eerily quiet throughout her testimony. It was almost as if we were all straining to hear her words.

Meanwhile, Forrest kept frantically making notes and passing them to his legal team.

Emily had been called as a witness for the prosecution, as she was able to give a clear picture of what Forrest was like out of the school environment. In this respect, she was the most independent of all the witnesses, who were much more affiliated with one side or the other. His parents had one view of him as he was their son, but as his estranged wife she had a clearer picture of him as a man.

Once Richard Barton had finished his questioning, it was Ronald Jaffa's turn again, and he immediately started asking questions and making observations that would undermine Emily. It quickly became evident that he was out to show she was a monster and that is why Forrest had been 'led astray'. Meanwhile, the note passing continued between Forrest and the rest of his team.

After a few minutes more, Emily broke down in tears. 'I can't do this!' she said, pointing at Forrest and his team as yet another note was passed over. 'It's all too distracting.'

At that point, Judge Michael Lawson, QC adjourned the session and we all sat in silence, wondering what was going to happen next. The judge then announced that he was going to let Emily give the remainder of her evidence from behind a curtain so that she wouldn't be distracted.

Ronald Jaffa was incensed, claiming that it should have been organised beforehand, but Judge Michael Lawson, QC simply wasn't interested – 'My courtroom, my rules,' he insisted.

And so the cross-examination continued, with Jaffa striking low blows against poor Emily, bringing up details about her private life and trying to suggest that she was mentally unstable. She stood firm throughout and corrected him on everything. Even if she had been a monster – which she obviously wasn't – that didn't give Forrest the excuse to do what he did to my daughter.

Finally, Jaffa's character assassination ended and Emily was allowed to step down. We never saw her in court again.

Detective Inspector Andy Harbour was next up and confirmed that he had been to France to bring Gemma back, and then it was chief inspector for child protection Mark Ling's turn to take the stand. There were no questions for either of them from the defence team as they were just there to confirm that all the police formalities had been followed.

Just before the court session ended for the day, I noticed that there was a bit of fuss going on between the legal teams about some document that the defence team hadn't yet received from the police. I wondered if perhaps this was the technicality that they were going to pull out of the hat.

But I had no need to worry: Richard Barton confirmed that they had the piece of paper to give to the defence team, and DI Neil Ralph was sent out to collect it. The defence team were obviously really clutching at straws if that was the only way they could win the case.

And that was that for the day. I felt exhausted and relieved that my day in court was over. Now I had to brace myself for the next day, when Forrest would finally take the stand ...

CHAPTER 38

DAY 8: WEDNESDAY, 19 JUNE

Now that the prosecution had concluded their questioning, it was time for the defence team to try and prove Forrest's innocence. Finally, we thought, we would find out what he had meant when he said that he would reveal 'the truth' about what had really happened between him and Gemma.

I desperately wanted to hear what he had to say. If he had pleaded guilty when first asked to enter a plea, none of us would have had to give evidence or go through the hell of the last few weeks. We had all been led to believe that he believed he had a strong reason to think he wasn't guilty of abducting my daughter. If he was so convinced of his innocence, today was the day for him to prove it.

Following our normal court-day routine of parking, meeting our friends, going for coffee and walking up the hill to the courthouse, we were ready for the big day. We sensed that the press knew it was going to be a significant day, too, and I felt that they were showing me more respect after I had given evidence the previous day. Maybe they had realised that I wasn't the chavvy mother the social media sites had been making me out to be, after all.

After we took our seats in the public gallery, the jury filed in, the legal teams assembled, and Forrest stepped into the dock. We all stood for the judge and there was an expectant hush as we took to our seats again and Ronald Jaffa stepped up to make an announcement.

'My client will not be taking the stand.'

What did he just say? Did I hear that correctly?

We all turned to each other, saying the same thing. Did he really just say that Forrest wasn't going to give evidence? Is that even allowed? As it slowly dawned on us that, yes, that was indeed what was happening, we sat there open-mouthed. We were speechless.

I don't know what Ronald Jaffa or the judge said next. All the blood had rushed to my head and I was absolutely fuming. How dare that man put my daughter through this hell if he had no intention of even taking the stand! At the very least, I was hoping that he would have had the tiniest piece of respect for Gemma and said that he did it because he cared about her, but he didn't even have the balls to do that. My entire family was shattered and he didn't offer a shred of an excuse for what he had put us all through.

Forrest had completely destroyed Gemma's childhood and robbed her of her last year at school and all the friendships and memories she should have enjoyed. He had used her for his own sexual needs and then refused to stand in the witness box to explain why.

There was no declaration of love, no apology, nothing.

If he had stood up there and said that he had done all of this because he loved Gemma, then at least there would have been some kind of emotional excuse to consider. It was quite obvious to me, though, that he didn't give a damn about her.

It seemed to me that Judge Michael Lawson, QC looked really annoyed. He told the jurors that they should come to their own conclusions as to why Forrest wasn't taking the stand.

I felt anger in its purest form in a way that I have never felt before. My hands were sweating, my heart was going nineteen to the dozen, my lips were tight and I could almost hear the blood rushing around my head. I couldn't take my eyes off him; I was absolutely raging.

For the defence team's next trick, they then read out six character references about Forrest. They had been written by his sister, his uncle, someone he used to work with and some old friends of his. I say 'friends', but they were obviously not exactly close, as none of them had bothered to come to court to support him.

Each statement took about five minutes to read out, and each said what a lovely, gentle person he was. They alluded to the fact that he had been locked in a bad marriage and had suffered with depression, and seemed to be suggesting he had almost been driven to find comfort elsewhere. Even if that was the case, it couldn't possibly justify what he did.

I can't speculate on what kind of marriage he and Emily had. I have been through a divorce myself and I know how hard it can be, but it didn't make me go out and commit a crime. The statements portrayed Forrest as someone who was weak and mentally disturbed and yet this was a man who came from a very supportive family, who was well-educated and had held down a good job. What they were saying just didn't add up.

Gemma was never once mentioned. If Forrest had said that he loved her, or that he wanted to marry her when he was able to, then perhaps, just perhaps, he would have had a tiny speck of an excuse. But there was nothing. The sum total of the defence was six pieces of paper; that was it. I kept trying to make sense of it. Why were we all sitting there?

All Forrest did was shuffle around a bit and wipe away a few crocodile tears.

Needless to say, when lunchtime came around, I was in a complete daze. The press pack seemed every bit as bewildered as we were. I remember turning to Chloe and saying, 'How the hell am I going to get Gemma through this, when the man she loves and has given up everything for hasn't got the balls to stand up and say he loves her?'

I was reeling. Gemma had done so much for Forrest by standing up in court and trying to clear his name, but he had given her no support whatsoever. He had merely used her as a tool in his defence, and was too spineless to stand up and prove that he loved her in return.

While his actions – or rather, lack of action – made me angry at first, I then began to feel sad for Gemma. I couldn't begin to imagine how she would feel when she found out that he had opted not to give evidence in his defence. All that heartache and sadness, and he wouldn't even stand up and say why he did it.

Then another thought struck me. Maybe now Gemma would start to see him for what he is, a shallow, self-centred excuse of a man, not the knight in shining armour who had whisked her away so they could be together. This was a man with no thought for anyone but himself.

Richard Barton did not pull any punches when he made his closing statement that afternoon. His words summed up everything that I felt about Forrest. They were brutal and hard for me to listen to – this was my daughter he was talking about, after all – but each thing he said was phrased to have the maximum impact on the jury.

Forrest, he said, was a paedophile who had groomed my daughter, and his actions were a gross abuse of trust: 'She trusted him with all her vulnerabilities and he was the figure of authority. He won't be the first figure of authority who someone gets a crush on and he won't be the last but part of the role of a figure of authority is that you do not take advantage of it … You do not expect your school to invite people to have sex with your underage daughter and you do not expect it to be the teacher.'

Some of his comments were directed at Forrest, some at the jury. Every word hit home hard.

'You do not have to decide whether he was a paedophile; you may consider, in the context of what he did, that is not an inappropriate label for him. It is about his desires to have that young sexual flesh, to satisfy his own carnal lusts,' he continued.

Some of the references to the evidence heard in court were almost too much to bear. Richard questioned how appropriate Forrest felt it was to send Gemma a photo of his 'naked torso, lying on a sofa with his hands in his underpants' and looked at him directly as he said: 'How did you feel when the fourteen-year-old student, this vulnerable girl, sent you pictures of her naked breasts? What did you do with those photos?'

His words were designed to shock but then again, make no

mistake about it, this was a shocking crime. As Richard said, this was not a case of Romeo and Juliet because they were not equal partners in what had happened and Forrest had organised the situation.

With every point he made, my stomach churned. I had flashbacks to that day when the police questioned me about the incriminating photos on Gemma's phone and Forrest's pathetic call to me in which he had practically begged me to stop my daughter 'being a pain'.

Richard also talked about Forrest's wife Emily: 'It is interesting to note the woman he chose to marry is a very young-looking, petite woman with her own vulnerabilities. What is that Jeremy Forrest finds attractive about young-looking, vulnerable women?

'There is a word for it. It's called grooming – being caring, being kind, being close, gaining confidence, gaining the trust of that person and then you can do what you want to do with them.'

Richard's closing statement lasted a good hour at least, and he delivered it masterfully. He ended by saying to the jury: 'I invite you to find him guilty as charged.'

Forrest's parents held on to each other and looked devastated by what they had just heard. I felt mentally exhausted; every point he had made was like a stab in the heart. It was a brilliant closing statement, but it had been so very difficult to listen to.

When it was all over, we walked out of the court and none of us knew what to say to each other. Someone suggested we go for a coffee, but it was all just too much.

Enough words. Enough emotion for one day.

CHAPTER 39

DAY 9:
THURSDAY, 20 JUNE

Despite Richard Barton's powerful closing statement, there was no guarantee that the trial would be over by the end of the week. We had no idea how long the jury would take to reach a verdict, so we had to start planning childcare in case it dragged on into a third week.

We knew that Ronald Jaffa would be giving his closing statement today. After that, there would be a statement from Judge Michael Lawson, QC, and then it would be time for the jury to consider its verdict. So it was back to court to hear what Forrest's lawyer had to say. Maybe today would be the day when he finally came up with the masterstroke that would prove Forrest's innocence.

When we arrived at court, Mark Ling and Neil Ralph pulled us aside to tell us that Gemma had turned up with the woman from Hertfordshire who had befriended her via Facebook. It was so upsetting for me to hear that she had chosen to attend court with a parasite she hardly knew. It also showed how vulnerable she was. First Forrest preys on her and now this woman.

As we took our seats in the public gallery, Gemma sat on the side where Forrest's parents always sat, but after a few minutes it became clear that the defence team didn't want her there and so she left the courtroom. I don't know what was said, but I felt so sorry for her, as I knew how much courage it must have taken for her to come in the first place. In any case, after a little while she came back into court again, clearly determined that she should be there.

The press later reported that we didn't look at each other, but that wasn't true. I looked over to her repeatedly that morning; it was, after all, the first time that I had seen her since she left home. I wanted to be sure she was OK, but all I got was dirty looks from the parasite. She didn't even know me but she had the nerve to think that I would be remotely interested in what her thoughts were. If I could, I would have scrambled across the benches and given Gemma a big hug. She looked so sad, lost and drained. I saw her and Forrest smile at each other. To me, it was as if he was still trying to intimidate her and keep her in his grasp.

Maybe now, finally, Ronald Jaffa would deal his ace card.

But no. In his closing statement, he claimed that Gemma was feeling suicidal, that Forrest had only gone to France to keep her safe, and that he was a good man. 'We humans find ourselves falling in love,' Ronald Jaffa said, 'even if we know it is inadvisable.'

That was the sum total of his defence – a few pathetic excuses for what Forrest had done. At no time did he give a reason why his client hadn't taken the stand, and he seemed to keep repeating himself as if he had run out of things to say.

People were getting fidgety in the court. Unlike Richard Barton, who had captured the evidence in such a clear, detailed way, Ronald Jaffa seemed to be floundering. 'I bet this is costing Forrest thousands,' I thought. 'What a waste of money.'

Forrest's relatives sat in the same anguished state as they had the day before, and I think everyone breathed a sigh of relief when Ronald Jaffa finished his closing statement. I kept glancing over at Gemma to see how she was taking it all. She looked so scared and vulnerable. It was an unbearable situation to be in. I can't imagine how she coped with hearing what was to come next.

Judge Michael Lawson, QC then began his summing-up. He talked to the jury directly and made reference to the fact that the information that Gemma gave the police in the September, as shown in the video footage presented to the court, was very different to the evidence that she subsequently gave in court, and instructed the jury to consider why she had done that.

It was clear to all of us that Gemma had been influenced about what to say. There was no doubt in my mind that the parasites had got to her and that the account she presented in court had been changed to support Forrest's defence.

Judge Michael Lawson, QC explained to the jury that they would have to consider that Forrest had acted 'out of necessity' and had taken her to 'prevent imminent death or serious injury' in order for them to acquit him. It was not, he added, Gemma's right to leave her parents' care without their permission – 'Questions of sympathy, or lack of it, or emotional responses to the evidence are not for now.'

Just before he concluded, Judge Michael Lawson, QC told the jury that he wanted them to make a unanimous decision, but that he would consider a majority verdict of 10-to-2 if they were unable to do so.

It was now over to the 8 men and 4 women of the jury to consider their verdict. All we could do was wait.

By this stage, it was about 11.30am. Mark Ling told us that he would call us as soon as the jury had reached their decision and so we headed out to our favourite tearoom. Naturally, we all believed it was obvious that Forrest was guilty, but what if the jury believed Gemma's courtroom testimony and disregarded her video evidence? I had to trust they would make the right decision and take on board everything that had been said.

After lunch, we wanted to stay close to the court, so we visited the hotel opposite for a cup of coffee. Someone mentioned to me that it was one of the hotels where Forrest had stayed with Gemma. Luckily, I didn't have time to dwell on that little piece of information, as at that moment my phone rang: the jury was back.

Chairs toppled and cups went flying as we all scurried back to court.

I noticed Gemma walking into court, too, and she looked really despondent. None of us could believe how quickly the jury had reached their decision. We later found out that they had taken only 40 minutes to reach a verdict, but that the judge had allowed them an additional hour for lunch.

Sitting in the public gallery, my heart was pounding. I could almost feel it in my throat. Judge Michael Lawson, QC looked at Forrest, then me, then Gemma. He then turned to the foreman of the jury and asked if a unanimous decision had been reached.

The foreman confirmed that it had, and the judge spoke again: 'How do you find the defendant?'

There was a short pause and we all held our breath. It seemed impossibly long to me, but it was probably no more than two seconds.

'Guilty.'

My head fell forward as the tension dropped away and I squeezed Paul's hand. I mouthed the words 'thank you' to the jury and then looked over towards Gemma. She was in floods of tears and was looking at Forrest. She said, 'I'm sorry', and he said, 'Don't worry, I'm fine.' Apparently, he then mouthed the words 'I love you' before he was taken to the cells.

Gemma blamed herself for what had happened. We had got the result that we hoped for, but this was only the start of the healing process to come.

Outside the court, the press were very keen to speak to me and there was almost a celebratory atmosphere. But I was in no state to celebrate – I was so upset about Gemma and the fact that she was there with that woman that I practically ran down the hill to get to the car and drive home. I just wanted to get home as quickly as possible – it was heartbreaking.

Shortly after the verdict was delivered, Portia Ragnauth, deputy chief crown prosecutor for CPS South East, read the following statement on the steps of Lewes Crown Court:

This case was one where a teacher was in a position of authority over a fifteen-year-old pupil and abducted her, taking her to another country. Not only did he breach the trust and confidence that all the parents at that school had placed in him, he also brought disgrace to his profession, who are trusted to look after the children in their care.

Forrest lied systematically about his relationship with the girl, repeatedly seeking to assure others who were concerned about the welfare of his victim that nothing untoward was going on between them.

Nothing detracts from the fact that this was an abduction. The law clearly states that it is an offence to remove a child from the care of their parents or lawful guardian without the adult's consent. Add to that the torment and anguish that the victim's family went through while they were gone.

None of us can begin to imagine how worried they were about her safety and wellbeing while she was gone for over a week, not knowing where she was or whether she was safe. It's a parent's worst nightmare to have their child abducted and to not know whether they will ever see them again.

Because Forrest abducted his victim to another country, this has been a complex case to bring to trial, which has been achieved by diligent work by our Complex Casework Unit and Sussex Police, along with assistance from our colleagues in France and the French courts.

Back home that night, there was quite a sombre mood in the house. We still had the sentencing to face and we had no idea how long Forrest would get. As the police had said, he had already spent so much time on remand, it was possible he could even walk free the next day.

CHAPTER 40

DAY 10: FRIDAY, 21 JUNE

Soon after we arrived at Lewes Crown Court on the Friday morning, Neil Ralph came over to let me know that Richard Barton wanted to see me upstairs.

I didn't know what to think. Inside the court, it was much busier than usual, with more people wanting to sit in the public gallery and significantly more press there than before. As Paul and I made our way upstairs, my mind was racing as to why Richard wanted to speak to us.

We were joined by Mark Ling and Andy Harbour. Richard explained that the judge had met with the defence and prosecution teams the day before and questions had been put to Forrest about the second charge of sexual activity with a minor. To my surprise and huge relief, Forrest had agreed for the charge to be included in this trial. It was as if a massive weight had been taken off my shoulders.

The formalities were explained to us. Judge Michael Lawson, QC would act as a magistrate while the charges of sexual activity with a child were put to Forrest for him to plead guilty, then the court would revert back to a Crown Court in order for the judge to pass sentence.

Trusted to keep these new developments to ourselves, we rejoined our friends and family in the courtroom. It was now packed, much fuller than it had been earlier in the trial. There were people we didn't know in the seats that we had occupied all week, but Matthew, the court usher, arranged for the upstairs balcony to be opened and moved them up there.

I couldn't believe how many people had come to ogle. It was like a cattle market. I couldn't understand why they wanted to see something like this. This was about my daughter, it had nothing to do with them.

Gemma wasn't in court that day, but I noticed nearly all of the team from Sussex Police who had worked on the case were there. For them, it was about closure as much as anything else, and I could see from their expressions that they were eager to hear the right result.

Forrest was brought up from the holding cells and I could see his mother and sister looking over anxiously, waiting for the inevitable. I could tell how upset they were. They had the added worry that Jim Forrest had fallen unwell the day before and been taken to hospital in an ambulance. I really felt for them.

Judge Michael Lawson, QC came into the courtroom and explained how the second charge of sexual activity with a minor was being added and that the court would revert to a magistrates' court for the duration of the committal proceedings. The clerk of the court then read out five charges of sexual activity with a minor.

With each charge, Forrest pleaded guilty.

Gemma had already admitted that they'd had sex and the Crown Prosecution Service had irrefutable evidence to prove it, so there was no way Forrest could attempt to deny it. He almost seemed to shrug off the significance of what he was saying as he pleaded guilty each time.

Then, with the court effectively turned back into a Crown Court, the judge was able to pass sentence on both crimes.

In his sentencing statement, Judge Michael Lawson, QC told Forrest that he had ignored the cardinal rule of teaching and had subjected our family to 'appalling distress'. He then added: 'Your behaviour over this period has been motivated by self-interest and has hurt and damaged many people – her family, your family, staff and pupils at the school, and respect for teachers everywhere. It has damaged you, too, but that was something you were prepared to risk.

'You now have to pay that price.'

The judge also referred to the fact that Gemma had been 'got at' to change her evidence. She had, he said, clearly received assistance in relation to what she should say.

Meanwhile, Forrest just sat there, looking blank.

Forrest was sentenced to four-and-a-half years in prison for the five offences of sexual activity with a child and one year for the offence of child abduction, to run consecutively. That meant a total of five-and-a-half years. Depending on good behaviour and other factors, he is unlikely to serve the full sentence, but Paul and I felt that justice had been done: the sentence felt right.

Forrest was also made to sign the sex offenders' register and banned from working with children for life.

I felt so relieved that it had all been brought to a head so quickly. As before, I didn't exactly feel like celebrating; this has never been about celebrating. That's not something I will ever be able to do.

Outside the court, it was mayhem. Neil Ralph read out a statement I had prepared for the press. In it, I thanked the team from Sussex Police who worked on Operation Oakwood, East Sussex Child Services, the French team, the media team and everyone else who had helped bring Gemma home and brought Forrest to justice.

Finally, we could leave. I couldn't wait to get home and see the children, and I began thinking about how I could rebuild my relationship with Gemma.

On the way home, I received a text from Kennedy High School, saying that the school had prepared a letter for the pupils to take home to their parents. It was about the day's verdict regarding a teacher and pupil at the school.

I couldn't believe what I was reading. How dare they write anything about my daughter without my consent? Gemma was no longer part of Kennedy High School and I wasn't going to allow them to try and justify their incompetence to unknowing parents.

I immediately rang the school and asked to speak to Mr Worship. 'What gives you the right to give out a letter about my child when you have done nothing to support her or my family? I am on my way to the school and I want a copy of that letter!' I told him.

Paul and I then drove straight to the school and Mr Worship was waiting for us. He showed us into his office and began to apologise for the text coming to us; we should have been removed from the group text mailing list. I had no qualms in telling him that I regarded it as just another demonstration of the school's total incompetence.

He gave me the letter and watched me as I read it. After a short while, I pushed it back to him. 'You do realise,' I said, 'that I hold you responsible for why this got out of control?' He replied, 'Yes, yes, I know, and I completely understand.'

Then it was Paul's turn. All the heartache of the day when Gemma went missing and the anguish of the weeks that followed came out in a flood. It had been brewing for nine months and he needed to vent his fury. He said he was absolutely disgusted by how the school had allowed this to happen. They'd been in the paper saying how much they'd done when really they'd done nothing. Worship just sat there and said, 'Yes, yes, I understand.' He couldn't offer us any more and repeated himself, so with that, Paul and I stood up and marched out of his office feeling determined that this wouldn't be the last they heard from us. We were so angry.

The extreme anger that I felt at that moment was to take over my life for the next few months. For a while, I wondered if it would ever go away. I reminded myself that I had suffered panic attacks for 10 years, but I'd been determined not to let them take over my life and, with help, had been able to overcome them. In the same way, I knew I would get through this feeling of rage that was taking control over me.

PART THREE

THE AFTERMATH

CHAPTER 41

HITTING THE HEADLINES AGAIN

On the Saturday morning, as I had expected, the court case was all over the papers.

In my victim impact statement, which was read out in court, I talked about the effect the case had had on my family and me. I said that Forrest had robbed Gemma of her childhood and that it felt like the daughter I knew was dead because of what he had done to her.

I hadn't prepared myself for how much the press would completely twist my words.

Somehow or other, a reporter had misquoted me and stories appeared, claiming that I had said 'My daughter is dead to me', as if I was saying that I wanted Gemma out of my life. It was totally untrue; the papers were totally misrepresenting what I had said. If I could have, I would have bought every newspaper printed and burnt every single copy.

That horrible line 'My daughter is dead to me' implied that I never wanted Gemma in my life again, which couldn't have been further from the truth. My actual words – 'I feel the daughter I knew has died and it upsets me beyond words' – were my way of saying that I felt that my delicate, innocent child had been taken away from me.

I knew that Gemma would see the headlines, too, so I immediately emailed her, warning her about what she might read and telling her that it wasn't true. She didn't get back to me, so I could only hope that she had read my email and had understood that I would never have said anything like that.

I was desperate to speak to the media and put the record straight. People needed to know that what they were saying simply wasn't true. Chloe, though, rightly said that it was beyond my control and persuaded me not to contact the papers.

Thankfully, not all the press repeated this horrible 'My daughter is dead to me' statement – the *Mirror*, for example, accurately reflected what I had said in my impact statement – and many of them went on to report on how Kennedy High School had failed Gemma and my family and explained how the East Sussex Local Safeguarding Children Board had begun a serious case review into the actions of the school.

The *Daily Telegraph*'s report included quotes from Lucy Duckworth, founder of the child protection charity See Changes – 'The repeated child protection failings at that school make it a complete shambles with clearly devastating consequences for the pupils in attendance there,' she said

– and a number of others quoted representatives from the NSPCC.

The *Daily Mail*, meanwhile, featured a front-page story with the headline, KIDNAP TEACHER GROOMED ME AT 13. Inside was an interview with Chloe Queen, the girl that Forrest had allegedly groomed at the school he taught at before he started at Kennedy High School. The police had told me about her during the course of their investigations, and I had hoped that her evidence might have been used in the trial, but I suppose the Crown Prosecution Service must have felt that it wasn't directly relevant to Gemma's case.

But there was one newspaper article, written by the television presenter Judy Finnigan, which particularly made my blood boil. It appeared in the *Daily Express* around a week after the trial ended.

In the piece, she criticised me for having made Gemma go to court. As if I had any say in the matter! It was the Crown Prosecution Service's decision who appeared before the court. She made all sorts of unfair assumptions about me as a parent and, because she was famous and in the public eye, I feared her comments would be taken as the truth.

I wanted to contact her to put the record straight and even considered sending her husband and fellow presenter, Richard Madeley, a message on Twitter, but I knew that Twitter posts were public and that it could potentially lead to even more bad press and Twitter trolls.

It was incredibly frustrating, but I knew I just had to let it go. Judy Finnigan is a mother herself and I would have hoped that she would have looked into my situation properly, rather than simply jump to conclusions. I remembered that her own daughter had once been the subject of some negative and unpleasant press coverage, so presumably she too had felt attacked as a parent. The fact that she was criticising me like this was very hurtful.

CHAPTER 42

FORREST'S SISTER IN THE SPOTLIGHT

After I stepped out of court on the last day of the trial, I was bombarded with interview requests and invitations to appear on every TV show under the sun, but I always declined. One paper had even said 'name your price' to me, but I had no interest in being part of the whole media circus. I knew the papers only wanted to know about the scandal and graphic details of what had happened between Forrest and Gemma. They weren't interested in the impact that his vile actions had had on my daughter or the rest of my family.

Money would never make up for what had happened to us. I thought about speaking to the press to put the record straight when they published things that were totally incorrect, but I knew I would never have any control over what they wrote and could have ended up endlessly fighting fires. I didn't want to become that kind of character who was constantly using the press to sound off.

It soon became evident, however, that Forrest's sister, Carrie Hanspaul, had other ideas …

On Tuesday morning, I switched on my TV and saw Carrie being interviewed by Lorraine Kelly on ITV's *Daybreak*. She claimed that Gemma was the love of her brother's life and said that he had been misunderstood. She went on to say that when he came out of prison, if he was to continue a relationship with Gemma, she would be welcomed into the family.

I couldn't believe what I was hearing; I was disgusted. Forrest's family weren't interested in Gemma. They had always made it plain that they wanted nothing to do with her. If they really believed he was in love with her, why did they have to wait until he came out of prison to accept her into their family?

Carrie Hanspaul also talked about how the school had left me seven messages that I had failed to return. If she had actually taken the trouble to ask the police about those so-called messages, she would have known that this wasn't the case. She was just using anything she could to try and deflect the blame from her brother. I can't blame her for being loyal to her family, but it was incredibly frustrating to hear her rake over things that were totally untrue.

Her publicity campaign continued. After *Daybreak*, she went on to appear on several other programmes, all the while trying to paint a better picture of her brother. I heard a rumour that the Forrest family had employed a PR company in a bid to get the media to portray him in a more favourable light. It will be interesting to see how it all plays out when he is released from prison.

Shortly after Forrest was sentenced, his family issued a statement to the press in which they talked about the impact the case had had on their family, but now Carrie Hanspaul was turning up in the papers talking about her brother as if he wasn't a convicted criminal, telling anybody who would listen that he really wasn't a paedophile. Any respect that I had had for that family went out of the window there and then.

My family and friends were just as disgusted as I was. They desperately wanted to speak to the media on my behalf and give my side of the story, but I wouldn't let them. I didn't want to become part of a public feud.

Thankfully, once Carrie Hanspaul had finished with her publicity campaign, she flew back to her home in the Middle East, and that was the last we heard of her.

But the newspaper coverage of Carrie's despicable claims about her brother and his supposed love for Gemma was by no means the last of the unpleasant stuff I had to read. A few days before Forrest was sent to jail, the TV presenter Stuart Hall was sentenced to 15 months in prison for a series of historic sex offences. The sentence was subsequently doubled to 30 months by the Court of Appeal and he has since been sentenced to a further two-and-a-half years in prison for two counts of indecently assaulting a girl.

Quite a lot of newspapers compared Hall's 15-month sentence to Forrest's five-and-a-half years and asked why there was such a huge difference. Underneath, I would read comments from people saying that Forrest and Gemma had been in love and, as a result, he should have been treated as leniently as Stuart Hall.

It was awful to read this sort of thing. I was outraged. Gemma was a child, Forrest was her teacher. How could they not see that Forrest had grossly abused his position of responsibility and the trust placed in him?

Why couldn't these people understand that, as Richard Barton said in his closing statement at the trial, Forrest had groomed a vulnerable young girl?

CHAPTER 43

BACK
TO WORK

A week after the trial was over, I went back to work full time. When you have been out of the nine-to-five routine for a while, it is really difficult to readjust to doing an eight-hour day's work and a two-hour commute each way. It was absolutely exhausting, but I was excited to be back in the thick of things, working on the company's process of modernisation.

My colleagues, as ever, were fantastic. Those who knew about the case were very respectful and never said anything about it, while the younger people I worked with seemed oblivious to any connections I had with the story. In a way, being back at work was an escape from what had been happening.

Gavin, my line manager, was great about the situation. He knew that I still had things at home that I had to deal with and he said he would allow me to have more time off, if I ever needed it. He knew my job wouldn't suffer because of it. I loved training the younger members of staff and inspiring them to work hard and be promoted in the company. It was really rewarding to see them doing so well.

At home, I had a great support network, which allowed me to go back to work. Paul or his parents would always look after Lilly whenever I had to go away overnight for work, my sister Charlotte and Max were very supportive and Lilly's nursery was really accommodating, too. As paranoid as I had been with Maddie and her male teachers, it was a comfort to me to know that there were no men working at the nursery. What had happened to Gemma had only made me more protective where my children were concerned. I would never have been able to sleep at night if I didn't know that I'd done everything I possibly could to keep them safe.

Over the days and weeks following the trial, I had some very big issues to work through. Firstly, my relationship with Gemma was going nowhere and she was still refusing to speak to me, which was breaking my heart. She was still living at Max's and still in touch with the parasites. On top of that, I had my family at home to consider, and my relationship with Paul was becoming strained – we were both so busy with our jobs, we were like ships that passed in the night. And then, of course, there was all the Forrest family stuff in the press to contend with and the prospect of the serious case review coming up. Throughout the court case his family were constantly talking to the press and looking forward to the outcome of a serious case review, which was going to occur at the end of the trial. This could only take place at end of the trial as they had to wait for the criminal case to be completed.

I was really struggling. It was as if I was being pulled in every direction. I kept thinking, 'At the end of this week I'll have a bit of breathing space' but that end seemed nowhere in sight.

I had read some people refer to the song 'Don't Stand So Close to Me' by The Police when they had commented on Gemma's story in the press. I had the song on my iPod, and one day when I was sitting on the train to work, I took the opportunity to really listen to it properly. Obviously, I had heard it many times in the past, but it had never truly resonated with me before. This time, I really concentrated on the words and I could hardly believe how familiar it all sounded – 'This girl is half his age ...'

Gemma's school prom was coming up soon. Although I had previously told Mr Worship that there was no way I was going to allow her to miss it, I knew that it wasn't going to be possible for her to attend. I realised we would just be asking for trouble if she went.

I had heard on the grapevine that some of Gemma's former schoolmates were blaming her for what had happened. They were saying that she had flirted with Forrest and that she had been the one to start their relationship. I knew it wasn't true, but it really hurt. She wasn't that sort of girl – she was far too into her music and creating websites, she would never have made a move on someone. She'd had a boyfriend in the past, but it was never anything serious. Yet from the moment she got back from France, she was called every abusive name under the sun.

Gemma had already decided that she didn't want to go anyway. I was told by one of her friends that she had heard some students say that they would boycott the prom if she was going, as they blamed her for what had happened. I myself had also heard this.

It was disappointing that the prom would be a no-go for her. I remembered when Lee had attended his own prom, all dressed up in a suit for the evening. I had thought at the time how special it was going to be for Gemma to have a new dress and her hair and make-up done, how excited she and her friends would have been, what kind of car we would arrange to get them there. Your school prom is one of those significant days of your teenage years that you hope to treasure forever. Sadly, in Gemma's case, it was to be another one of those special memories that she had been denied.

During this time she was still friendly with some of her old classmates from Kennedy High School and I became great friends with one of the girl's mums. The girl's mother was able to keep me updated on how Gemma was getting on, and I was pleased to know that she had an older female figure in whom she could confide if she needed to. I didn't expect any information about Gemma to be relayed back to me, it was just comforting to know that there was a 'mum' there for her if ever she needed one.

Every day, I kept up the text messages to Gemma, hoping that one day we would be able to get our relationship back on track. It was what I wanted more than anything in the world.

I knew that Gemma needed space, but I needed her to know that I would always love her and would always be her mum. Every day as I wrote her another text and hit the send button on my phone, I hoped that I would finally get through to her how much she meant to me.

CHAPTER 44

THE PARASITE IS ARRESTED

Towards the end of June, around a week after the trial ended, Mark Ling got in touch with me. Acting on instructions from Judge Michael Lawson, QC, he and Neil Ralph were about to travel up to Hertfordshire to talk to the parasite who had accompanied Gemma to court on the day of the verdict.

Judge Michael Lawson, QC had questioned the evidence that Gemma had given in court and had been concerned that it had strayed so much from her original police interview. He said there was reason to believe that someone had contacted Gemma to get her to change her story and that she had been coached on what to say in court.

Even though Judge Michael Lawson, QC didn't know Gemma at all, he could tell that what she said in court didn't sound like her own words, and I felt vindicated that I wasn't the only one who believed she had been 'got at' to change her story. He was so perceptive and I was greatly relieved to find that he had picked up on the fact that the words she had been saying weren't her own.

At the end of the sentencing hearing, he asked Richard Barton if he had any evidence of collusion. When Richard had confirmed to him that Sussex Police suspected some kind of foul play, the judge said: 'I will expect to see them back in my court.'

So off Mark Ling and Neil Ralph went to Hertfordshire ...

I wish I could have been a fly on the wall when they finally caught up with the parasite. As far as I was concerned, what she had been doing was just a continuation of Forrest's grooming. Gemma had confided in this woman about how she was feeling and she in turn had been feeding back information to the press and Forrest's family. On top of that, of course, she had visited Forrest in prison and made numerous telephone calls to him.

The police had asked me to collate evidence of the parasite's relationship with Gemma and give them a statement. Gemma's phone bills were in my name, so I could see exactly how many calls she had made to 'Hertfordshire woman', while the police were able to track the calls that she in turn had made to Gemma.

Needless to say then, the parasite had plenty of explaining to do when Mark Ling and Neil Ralph eventually turned up on her doorstep.

Her husband and her employers were completely oblivious to the double life that she had been leading. She was arrested on suspicion of perverting the course of justice and was released on bail while the police continued their investigations.

Her bail agreement stipulated that she must keep away from Gemma, but I heard from sources other than the police that she got in touch with her via social media sites. I had seen that Gemma had replied to a tweet from someone with a name that I didn't recognise, and I was convinced it was her because of the language that she used.

To this day, Gemma and I stay away from this subject, but she has gradually come to understand why I was trying to protect her from this woman.

'Hertfordshire woman' had been desperate to be part of Gemma and Forrest's so-called love story, but I just wanted her to go back to her sad life and leave my daughter alone. I so hoped Gemma would one day see how this warped woman had cruelly manipulated the situation.

Around a month later, Mark Ling got back in touch to tell me that the police were continuing with their investigation and that it could potentially lead to another court appearance for Gemma and me. Alternatively, he said, they could drop the case and let her off with a warning.

I really wanted this parasite to be punished, but I couldn't bear the thought of everything being dragged through court again. After giving the matter a lot of thought, I eventually decided to ask the police to drop the case. I hoped that the very fact that they had caught up with her and warned her would stop her contacting Gemma again.

I looked into seeing whether I could take out an injunction against the woman to make her stay away from Gemma, but this would have had to have come from Gemma herself, and I knew that would never happen. I just had to hope that their 'friendship' would burn out over time.

Since then, both parasites have shown their true colours.

'Shrine woman' turned really nasty when she discovered that Gemma was getting on with her life, and started calling her all sorts of disgusting names. Meanwhile, 'Hertfordshire parasite' started playing mind games, posting cryptic messages on Twitter, knowing full well that Gemma would understand what they meant. When that didn't work, she then went on to target Gemma with abuse, as it dawned on her that the hold she had on my daughter was slipping away.

CHAPTER 45

THE REUNION

Throughout this period, I kept up my daily text messages to Gemma. To my delight, on Monday, 1 July 2013, she finally agreed to meet me.

I don't know exactly what it was that finally triggered a response, but I didn't care; I was beyond ecstatic to hear from her. I knew that I couldn't afford to get ahead of myself, and that I would have to play everything carefully so that I didn't jeopardise further communication between us, but I was so relieved that we could finally start to mend our broken relationship.

We agreed that Lilly, Gemma and me would go for dinner at the local Harvester restaurant and arranged that I would pick her up from Max's at 6pm. As I was getting ready for our 'date', I remember feeling so nervous and excited about the prospect of spending a few hours with her after all this time. On top of that, I had the added challenge of trying to keep Lilly awake for long enough for Gemma to see her. Usually I start Lilly's bedtime routine at around 6pm, but on this occasion I wanted to try and keep her alert, and so I was singing my head off in the car on the way to Max's.

When I got there, Gemma came out of the house and got into the back of the car to sit next to her baby sister. It was so wonderful to see them together again. I knew that Gemma had been really missing Lilly and it was lovely to watch her make a massive fuss over her. Seeing them together like that really helped defuse any kind of awkwardness that there might have been between us. I just quietly drove along, not wanting to break that special moment between them.

When we got to the restaurant, Gemma took Lilly out of her car seat and hugged her really tightly. Again, I didn't want to interrupt their moment, so I just hung back.

I could see that the last few months had really taken their toll on Gemma. She looked so tired. She was still my beautiful daughter, of course, and she looked so lovely in her pretty summer dress, but under the surface I could see she was drained. The trial had obviously had a huge impact on her: she looked like she had the weight of the world on her shoulders.

I knew that there were subjects that I had to avoid and I made a promise to myself that I would try not to bring up the subject of the trial. I had to treat her with kid gloves. If I wanted to move forward and have any kind of relationship with my daughter, I told myself, I had to respect everything that she said. I wouldn't rant or lay my own feelings on the line: tonight was all about Gemma.

She didn't want to eat, so we had a drink together and caught up on family stuff – how Alfie was doing, what Lee was up to and so on – and talked about her exams. I was so pleased to hear that she thought that they were going well. It was a lovely, normal night that any parent and teenage child might have.

For about an hour, we just chatted away about this and that, but we were both aware that there was a massive elephant in the room. We were talking about everything under the sun except the trial. I know I had promised myself that I wouldn't mention it, but I couldn't help myself. Finally I plucked up the courage and asked her direct: 'How did you feel about being in court?'

Gemma was absolutely fine about talking about it. She told me how she had felt weird having all her family and my friends there hearing about what had gone on. Of course she had known that it was all going to come out in the newspapers eventually, but she said she hadn't wanted them to actually hear the words being said out loud. She also wanted to know why I had felt the need to be there every day. 'You're my daughter and the case was about you,' I told her. 'Why would I be anywhere else?'

We were both speaking very calmly and there was no bad feeling. I asked her why she hadn't wanted to go back to court after she had given evidence, and she explained that she didn't want to hear everyone talking about her. Also, she knew she would have had to contend with the press pack every day, even with the court order that was in force.

After a little while I asked her if she had been in contact with Forrest's family. She told me that she hadn't and, while I didn't really believe her, I decided to leave it at that. There was no point in me pushing it – she knew exactly how I felt about him and their relationship.

I wanted to let the conversation flow rather than hound

her with questions. We talked a little about how her feelings about what had happened might change with the passage of time, and I reiterated that I would always be there for her, should there be anything she needed.

In total we were together for about three hours, after which I dropped her back at Max's. We could have talked for much longer, but I needed to get Lilly properly tucked up in her cot, as she had been asleep for the whole time we were in the restaurant. Those three hours we had together at that Harvester had been enough for us to start rebuilding bridges. I knew we still had a long way to go, but I was so, *so* relieved that we were finally talking again.

Paul's face lit up when I got back home. He could tell how happy I was about talking to Gemma again. He said: 'That's the first time I've seen a genuine smile on your face for ages!'

I then posted a picture of Gemma and Lilly on Facebook with the words 'A great day!' Almost immediately, I started receiving lots of lovely messages from friends and family – they all knew how much it meant to me to have spent time with Gemma. I hadn't told anybody that I was going to meet her in case she cancelled, so it was great to now be able to tell everyone about it. One friend posted a comment that particularly touched me: 'It's good to see the adorable mermaid and the adorable princess reunited.'

I was determined to keep working on rebuilding our relationship, and continued sending Gemma text messages, encouraging her to come over to the house for dinner and so on. But I knew I had to be patient – I couldn't pressurise her, I had to let her do things on her own terms and at her own pace.

One day, after we had been out shopping together, she came

back to the house with me. She was feeling really tired, so she went upstairs to her room for a nap. It was reassuring to know that she felt comfortable being there, but I didn't put any pressure on her to stay and dropped her back at Max's afterwards. It was great that it was all moving in the right direction, but I was still walking on eggshells, mindful we still had a long way to go.

Little by little, I could see that Gemma was learning to live without Forrest and was rebuilding her life. I heard through her schoolfriend Rosie's mother that she had started to see more of her friends and was meeting new people. I wasn't expecting Gemma to embark on another romance or anything, but I was glad that she was having fun again and doing all of the usual teenage stuff.

One day, Gemma was over at the house and she told me that she, Rosie, Lee and Lee's girlfriend Natalie had booked tickets to go to Reading Festival. It was going to be her first festival where she would be staying over, so of course I was a little concerned and did my usual 20 questions about how safe it would be there and so on. Typical me: paranoidmum. com!

But as there would be four of them there together, I felt reassured everything would be OK, especially as one of them was her brother. I was a teenager once myself – I knew what kind of things went on at festivals, and I knew that they would all come back filthy and exhausted, but Gemma was sixteen now and I was happy for her to go and finally have some fun.

The festival took place over the August Bank Holiday weekend and Paul, Lilly and I were staying with his parents in Somerset while they were there; Maddie and Alfie were spending the weekend with Max. Driving back home on the

Monday, I received a text message from Gemma. She wanted to know if it would be OK if she stayed with us that night.

I was so thrilled. Barely a second later, I was furiously typing away on my phone: 'Of course you can!'

Then came another text message: 'Also, would you mind if I dye my hair?' Again, I said that was fine – I was so delighted that she had even asked. I would probably have agreed to a party, too, if she had asked for one!

A little while later, I received another text message: 'Had a bit of an accident with the hair dye'. 'Uh-oh, here we go,' I thought. When I got back to the house, Gemma had an expression on her face like she was five years old again and I had caught her playing with my make-up and jewellery. She looked at me with big sad eyes – 'I'm so, so sorry, Mum ...'

Upstairs, the bathroom looked like a crime scene. There was hair dye everywhere – up the walls, along the side of the bath, all over the sink. But what could I do? There was a time when I would have gone mental with her – it was a brand new house, after all – but it was just one of those things.

In a way, though, it was good to be living those typical teenage moments again, and the expression on Gemma's face told me that underneath everything, she was still my little girl. It might sound crazy, but it was a moment to treasure.

After that, she never left. My precious mermaid was back.

I remained very careful about what I said to her, as we were still in different mindsets. I tried to take things slowly and treat her like a delicate china cup. It wasn't so easy – Gemma had said some very hurtful things to me over those weeks – but I was terrified that she would leave again.

I felt very defensive if anyone said anything remotely critical about Gemma. I wanted her to have her own space to get through everything. In hindsight, though, I wonder if perhaps I gave her too much space.

I have always set clear boundaries for my kids, and I have really learned how important they are over the last year or so. It is no good me trying to be their best friend all the time. After what had happened to Gemma, though, I didn't always know what to do for the best. Whenever she would get particularly irritable or angry, I would seek advice from Sarah, who would invariably tell me that it was perfectly normal behaviour for someone in her situation.

When the trial was over, lots of people said to me, 'Well, at least things can go back to normal now'. If only! What happened to Gemma feels like a life sentence that will never go away. Every aspect of our lives has been affected. Through my research into child abuse, I have learned that there is no way to know for certain how long it will take for my daughter to truly come to terms with what has happened to her. It could take her years.

CHAPTER 46

MOVING FORWARD

Paul and I had been due to get married at the end of June 2013. We had planned to have the party in a beautiful village in Somerset called Dunster, where Paul had grown up and gone to school. With its thatched roofs and pretty higgledy-piggledy streets, it really is chocolate-box pretty and the perfect setting for a country wedding.

We had got quite far down the line with all the arrangements – I had even bought the table centrepieces – but we knew that we had to put everything on hold once we found out that the trial was definitely going ahead. I was really disappointed, but I knew it was for the best. We would just have to wait until the trial was over and done with.

By the time the trial came to an end, though, we just didn't feel like we were in a place to celebrate anything. Weddings are meant to be about family and everyone coming together in happiness, but our family was so fractured and there was still so much hurt between us.

Relations between Paul and I were sometimes strained. It was a very difficult time for us. He used to get annoyed with me that I would allow Gemma to speak to me the way that she did and that I let her have the upper hand, but I was so worried that she would run away again. I knew I was treating Gemma differently to her brothers and sisters, but I didn't know how else to behave with her.

I got a lot of help and advice through organisations such as Enough Abuse and the NSPCC. At the end of the trial, with the case now closed, the police said their goodbyes, and the social services told us that we wouldn't need them anymore. With so many of my support networks slipping away, I felt like I was falling without a parachute. It was a very tough time for all of us. I tried my best to keep my head down and do what I thought felt right.

Then, in August, the most fantastic thing happened – Gemma got her exam results and it turned out that she had done incredibly well! I was over the moon, as I'd had no expectations at all. I have always told my children that all they can do is try their best, but I had assumed that with all the pressure that she was under – and the fact that some of her exams would be taking place at the same time as the trial itself – that Gemma would have to do re-takes. Instead, she aced all of them!

Over the course of the summer, we registered a new temporary name for Gemma, as we didn't want her to be recognised as 'that runaway schoolgirl' when she began at her new college in the autumn. I had changed the children's names before when I married Max, so I knew that it was a relatively straightforward process and I met with the college's head of student services to explain the situation.

Gemma's first few weeks at her new college went very smoothly. I had been slightly concerned that she was taking on too much, as she had decided to study for four A-levels, but she seemed to be doing really well. By November, though, it became clear that she was struggling with the workload.

We arranged a meeting with all of the relevant heads of department. Gemma had decided that she wanted to drop two subjects, which made sense to me after everything she had been through. After all, she could always take on further subjects when she felt more able.

When I got to the meeting, though, one of her tutors seemed to really take against me. I tried to explain the situation, and his response was along the lines of, 'You can't use that as an excuse'. Luckily, Vikkie, the head of student services, stepped in and said that she didn't think it would be an issue.

The matter was quickly resolved – for the moment anyway ...

CHAPTER 47

RELIVING THE PAST YEAR

In September 2013, I was interviewed as part of the serious case review that had been set up by the East Sussex Local Safeguarding Children Board.

I had known for a while that I would be involved, but I was still very anxious about it. I knew that it would be a harrowing experience for me to have to remember all the details of what went on, but I also knew that the review might help me finally get some answers about why Kennedy High School had not done anything to prevent Forrest abusing my daughter.

Before the trial took place, I had received a letter from the man who would be writing the report, Kevin Harrington, inviting me to be interviewed. Kevin is an eminent, independent expert on health and social care, who has written a number of other serious case reviews over the years, including one concerning Tia Sharp, the twelve-year-old girl who was murdered by a former boyfriend of her mother's in August 2012. Gemma was also contacted and asked if she would like to contribute to the report, but she didn't want to know. As far as she was concerned, it was over and done with; she just wanted to move on. I totally understood – she'd had enough of what everyone was saying about it and I didn't blame her for taking that attitude.

Come the day of the interview, I was really worried about having to dredge over everything again. I hated the idea of being in the spotlight again and dreaded all the questions that might be going through their minds. Would they be wondering why I didn't know what had been going on? Once again, I felt like the worst mum in the world.

The interview took place at the offices of the Department of Child Services in Eastbourne and was conducted by Kevin Harrington and a representative from the health service. It lasted a good couple of hours and, despite feeling nervous about it, it felt good to get everything off my chest. There had been so much negative press and conjecture, I was grateful to be given the opportunity to put the record straight.

I told them everything I knew about the circumstances leading up to Gemma's disappearance. There was so much I wanted to tell them and it felt like a huge weight was lifted off my shoulders. They just let me talk and talk.

One of the subjects that came up was Gemma's health, and again I was asked about her so-called bulimia and self-harming issues. I made a point of talking about Gemma's existing health issues and I noticed the two of them nodding to each other. I felt that they could see I was telling the truth. It was so reassuring to know that my side of the story was being taken on board.

At the end of the interview I thanked them and they told me that what I had said tallied with their own information. Afterwards, I remember standing at the top of the stairs outside the office and taking a long, deep breath. After all this time thinking I must be the world's worst mum, it looked like I would finally be vindicated.

The review was due to be published before the end of the year and so it would be a while yet before I would hear its conclusions. In the meantime, with a new term at school for Maddie and Alfie, Gemma at college and little Lilly at nursery, it was all back to normal for us at home.

Of course, I say 'normal', but the truth was I was still struggling to hold it all together. I continued to find it incredibly draining working full-time, looking after Paul and the kids, and dealing with Gemma's moods. To be honest I didn't have the time to fit in counselling for myself but I didn't hold it against anyone – there was just too much going on.

CHAPTER 48

MORE SAD GOODBYES

In November 2013, one of my best friends Chloe moved to Australia as she had a fantastic new job. I was heartbroken that she was going to live so far away, especially after what we had been through together. She had been an absolute rock throughout the whole of the Forrest saga, and I honestly do not think I would have got through it without her. I was dreading saying goodbye.

We had worked at the same company for many years, so I volunteered to give her a great send-off. I booked a very grand country hotel and arranged an amazing black-tie party for around 65 guests. We really pushed the boat out – the hotel had stunning grounds and we had a big hog roast and a disco. It was such a great evening, the first in an awfully long time that I could remember laughing and having fun, but I kept on bursting into tears as well. Chloe had been the best friend that anyone could ever dream of.

I couldn't bear the thought of her leaving. She kept saying, 'I'm not dead, you know! We still have the phone and Skype, and you can always come and visit.' But it still felt like I was losing my right arm. On the day she left, we kept in contact all the way to the airport, and I even tracked her flight online to make sure she landed safely.

She was right, of course; we do still speak to each other regularly. I worry, though, that I will never be able to repay her for all the help, time, love and support she gave me. Thank you just doesn't even begin to cover it.

And there were more goodbyes to come. Mum and my sister Charlotte had decided to move up to Derbyshire to live near my other sister Annette, and were planning to start a new business up there. Gemma had previously been so close to the pair of them, and it broke my heart to see the way they had grown further and further apart since the trial.

I was gutted that they were moving. It felt as if all these layers of support that I'd had before were just dissolving around me. First it had been the police and Sarah the social worker, then Chloe, Mum and Charlotte. Then, shortly afterwards, I found out that Vikkie from the college would also be leaving. I felt so very alone.

I didn't feel I could talk to anyone at home about it; I didn't want to burden Paul with any more of my woes. He had been so wonderful these past months and I knew I had to try to hold things together at home. I was a mum in the morning, a manager during the day, then a mum again in the evening, and I didn't feel I could really be vocal about how I was feeling. The only time when I could really let go was when I was in the car on the way to and from work. I remember one time I had to pull over as I was crying so much: I felt so empty, life was such a struggle.

The situation with Gemma was extremely challenging at times. She still didn't want to have anything to do with our extended family. When they would come round to visit, I would try to force the issue and make her spend time with them. I know that she thought they were angry with her, but I wanted to make her see that nobody blamed her for any of this.

In November, a little while after our meeting with her tutors, Gemma decided that she wanted to leave college. She really wasn't enjoying it there and wanted to try and get an apprenticeship in graphic design.

I was concerned about it, but I knew that she would make sure she had something lined up before she left. I've never put any pressure on Gemma to achieve high grades or get a flashy job, but she has always been very ambitious and worked hard. She very quickly lined up an apprenticeship and had started work within weeks of leaving college. It underlined how determined she was.

Shortly after this, Lee asked me if I would mind if he moved in with his girlfriend Natalie. I was absolutely delighted. Natalie is a beautiful young woman and I couldn't wish for anyone better for him. I thought it was so sweet that he asked me, as he obviously knew that it was another big life stage for me to have to face. They were only going to be five minutes away, so I knew I would still see them all the time, and I was so happy for them to take the next step.

Meanwhile, there was Christmas to look forward to. There were going to be fewer of us than ever this Christmas Day. It was Max's year to have Maddie and Alfie staying with him, and Lee was going to be at Natalie's parents, so it would just be me, Paul, Gemma and Lilly at home. It was certainly going to be much quieter than usual.

At that stage, my relationship with Gemma was very much on her terms. I never questioned her when she was distant from us, as I had learned that if I put any pressure on her she just wouldn't speak to us at all. Occasionally, though, she would open up to me, and it was around this time that she told me that she had met with Forrest's parents. Gemma knew I wouldn't have been happy about her doing that – I felt that for all the time the Forrests were staying in contact with her, they were just adding to the guilt that she felt about the whole situation – but I didn't give her a hard time about it or push her away.

I understand that Forrest's parents had to adapt to having a son in prison – I can't imagine what it must be like not being able to see your child or contact them whenever you want to. But having Gemma see their grief firsthand was just prolonging the damage to her that their son had already caused.

CHAPTER 49

ANSWERS AT LAST

In December 2013, a week or so before the serious case review was due to be published, I was invited to a meeting with Kevin Harrington and one of his colleagues. I asked for Paul and Gemma to be allowed to come along, too, and was so relieved when Gemma said that she would like to be there because it meant that she would be able to hear the information directly and there would be no doubt about what was said.

Previously, when I had relayed information from the police to Gemma before the trial, she had accused me of only telling her half the story, and it had caused a lot of heartache for the pair of us. I had learned that if there was anything significant regarding the case that she needed to be told about, it was better to get the person responsible to tell her directly rather than have me relay information. That way, she could be certain she got all the facts.

The meeting was taking place in order to inform us of the top-line messages that would be appearing in Kevin Harrington's report, so that there would be no nasty shocks for us when it was officially published. On the morning we were due to meet, I was my usual nervous self.

Now, finally, I would be hearing the truth about what the school should have done to stop what happened.

As before, we all met up at the offices of the Department of Child Services in Eastbourne, and I could see straight away that Kevin Harrington was intrigued to meet Gemma. Given that he knew so much about her, it was only natural that he would be curious to meet her face to face. I suppose it was like fitting the final piece into a jigsaw puzzle – he knew so much about her before, but meeting her in person completed the picture.

We all sat down and eagerly awaited the findings. One by one, a damning list of failures was outlined to us.

In summary, the report found the following:

- Kennedy High School had been protecting Forrest, not Gemma, and treated him as the victim rather than her.
- The school had child safeguarding policies in place, but teachers failed on several occasions to act upon them.
- The school failed to notify the correct authorities in the first instance and repeatedly dismissed concerns raised by other pupils.
- School staff never spoke to Gemma in a way that was supportive.
- The school failed to update me as a parent and denied me the opportunity to help Gemma.

It was one disgraceful revelation after another. The report found that staff at the school had repeatedly dismissed evidence from pupils revealing that Forrest might be an abuser and adopted instead a 'default position' of 'intuitively supporting him as a colleague' and viewing him as 'the victim'.

They had effectively put Forrest's needs first and had completely failed to follow the correct procedures. Forrest had been spoken to on numerous occasions by various members of staff, and yet the situation had been allowed to continue.

Also – and this information was key to me – the report shed some light on the school's claims that they had contacted me seven times. Forrest's sister had also mentioned this when she had been interviewed on TV, but I knew this to be untrue.

The report revealed that, while the school claimed to have left me several messages, their phone logs proved that they didn't stay on the line long enough to hear my answerphone message and leave their own details. The log showed that each of the calls was only 30 seconds long, yet my answerphone message at the time was 28 seconds long, so they would have needed to have talked pretty damn fast to have left a message.

Yes, they called me – and yes, I subsequently returned their calls – but I never ignored seven messages. Like any other person, I may miss calls or forget to return messages in the first instance, but I would never have ignored seven messages, especially when they were about one of my children.

If the school believed that there was something going on to be concerned about, they should have left full messages for me and notified the appropriate authorities as soon as the rumours started.

The whole time that we were hearing this information, Gemma just sat there in silence, nodding and taking it all in. I wouldn't have wished the situation on my worst enemy, but I breathed a sigh of relief that finally we were getting the answers that we needed.

I had always assumed my daughter would be safe while she was at school. How wrong I was! As Kevin Harrington's report showed, they had failed Gemma miserably. It was inexcusable.

Back at home after the meeting, I called my close family and friends to tell them about the report's findings. Like me, they were all relieved to hear that everything was going to be out in the open, but they too were disgusted that the school hadn't done a proper job of protecting Gemma. In a way, I suppose I had hoped that it wasn't the school's fault and that everything that had happened was down to Forrest and his twisted needs alone, but it turned out that the school was at the heart of the problem.

Gemma was very quiet and didn't want to talk about it. She needed time to process the information. As hard as that was for me, I had to take a step back. She knew I would always be there for her if ever she wanted to talk about it.

A couple of days later, Douglas Sinclair, the head of child safeguarding in East Sussex, got in touch to see how we were all feeling about the report. He talked me through the process of how it would be released and how the press might pick up on it. Already he had some interview requests from some of the national newspapers, but I told him that I didn't want to comment.

Douglas added that he would arrange for the report to be sent to me on the morning of its publication, so that I would have a chance to read all 46 pages of it in full in advance of its release.

Come the morning of Monday, 16 December, I was dreading looking out of the window and seeing hordes of reporters again. Thankfully, there was nobody there and everyone went off to school and work as normal. I had a day off in case there were any unexpected repercussions from the report and I kept an eye on the television for when it hit the local and national news.

Mr Worship, the executive head of Kennedy High School, appeared on the early evening news on ITV to talk about the report and it seemed to me as if he was just reading a script. After a blink-and-you'd-miss-it apology, he went on about how the school had made great steps to change its safeguarding policies. The whole thing was just pathetic and I was furious that he was allowed to use this damning serious case review as some kind of PR stunt for the school.

But the reporter on the local BBC News programme gave him a much harder time than her counterpart on ITV and didn't allow him to stick to his script about how great the school was now. She asked him precisely the sort of questions that I wanted answers to. Why was it allowed to happen in the first place, and why was it permitted to go on for so long?

He grudgingly admitted the school's failings, but was also quick to point out that the police and social services had also been criticised for their part in the whole sorry affair. This was true, but the report's criticisms of them were far more minor, as he well knew.

A week or so later, I heard from Douglas Sinclair again, saying that Mr Worship wanted to write me a letter. When the letter arrived, once again he glossed over an apology and wrote about all the steps that the school had taken to improve their safeguarding policy. Like I was interested! Don't get me wrong, I would never want what happened to Gemma to happen to anyone else, but I would have appreciated more than just a three-line apology. I wanted him to really focus on the damage that had been done and the failings of his school.

I discussed the contents of the letter with Douglas Sinclair, who told me that Mr Worship had been in touch with him again and would now like to write to Gemma. I said he could – on condition that he wasn't to go on about how great the school was now. Gemma is not stupid, she would have known he had only made all of these improvements as a result of what had happened to her.

Luckily, when his letter arrived, Mr Worship had followed my request and Gemma received a full apology.

CHAPTER 50

MORE BATTLES TO FIGHT

As I had expected, Christmas 2013 was a very low-key affair. I remember waking up early on Christmas morning while everyone else was still asleep and stepping out into the garden. It was all so eerily quiet, and I stood there lost in my thoughts, wondering if we would ever be able to have a 'normal' Christmas again.

We had made the house look nice, and I hadn't scrimped on presents, but it just all felt flat somehow. It came and went almost like any other day. Thankfully, Boxing Day was much better – all the children came over and it felt much more like our typical family Christmas. New Year's Eve, on the other hand, was a real non-event. Gemma went out with some friends, so Paul and I put Lilly to bed and saw in 2014 watching Jools Holland on TV. After all the stress of the trial and the hurt and upset with Gemma, neither of us wanted to celebrate. All we wanted was for things to get back to normal. But as I have come to realise through all of this, just as we had got over one hurdle, another one would come along for us to deal with ...

During the trial, I was approached by a woman from an independent production company who said that she was making a documentary about teacher–pupil relationships for Channel 4. I told her that I wasn't in the least bit interested in getting involved – I was still in the process of understanding why all this had happened in the first place, after all – but some time later she got in touch again to see if I would reconsider.

Once again, I said no. I had no interest at all in being involved with the programme. How could I talk about something I didn't even understand myself? I had received a number of offers to sell my story and appear on TV, but I declined them all. Don't get me wrong, the money offered would have made a real difference to my family, but I couldn't face the idea of making a profit out of what happened to Gemma. As I have said before, I am only writing this book so that I can give my side of the story.

But I knew the documentary was going ahead whether or not I wanted to be part of it. I tried to see if I could get it stopped, but all of the information was already in the public domain and there was nothing I could do about it as long as the programme-makers adhered to the court order.

The programme was called *Sexting Teacher* and aired on Channel 4 on Tuesday, 18 February 2014. It focussed on three relationships: Gemma and Forrest's; another girl who had run off with her teacher and had a relationship with him for a few years; and a third teacher who was found guilty of sex offences but insists to this day that it was all lies.

Watching the programme was surreal to say the least. Channel 4 claimed that it was serious exploration of teacher–pupil relationships in the age of social media, but the reconstruction of Gemma's story was disgraceful. The actress portraying her seemed much older than her and behaved much more provocatively than she ever did. The way she was dressed didn't ring true at all – the programme-makers had obviously seen various different pictures of Gemma and pieced them all together into something that just wasn't her. They tried to piece it all together like a jigsaw puzzle but they put the pieces in the wrong places.

I hated the music they used, too – it was like a cheesy eighties pop video and made the whole thing seem like some tacky teenage romance, rather than a serious and responsible look at the issues of sexual relationships between teachers and their pupils. It was meant to be a documentary, but it just came over as some kind of Mills & Boon adaptation. Worst of all, Forrest was portrayed as a nice guy who was trapped in a loveless marriage and couldn't help himself getting involved.

I was furious at the way the whole issue had been portrayed. Gemma watched it upstairs – I can only think she was too embarrassed to watch it with me and Paul in the sitting room – but I knew she was fuming about it, too, as she later wrote a number of posts about it on social media.

The following day, I wrote an official letter of complaint to Channel 4. I also spoke to my solicitor about it, but I was told that there was nothing that I could do about it unless the programme-makers had actually broken the law.

The programme-makers clearly had no interest in the real issues. *Sexting Teacher* did nothing but add to the fiction that this was some kind of modern-day Romeo and Juliet story.

They even hinted that the 'romance' might continue when Forrest is eventually freed from prison.

In my letter to Channel 4, I asked question after question about why the story hadn't dealt with what actually happened – the fact that Forrest had groomed my daughter from the age of thirteen – and why they hadn't asked any child protection organisations to comment or mentioned the teachers' code of conduct. All of the legalities were glossed over to make way for the more salacious details, such as Gemma and Forrest having sex in a car or checking into hotels together.

I received a reply from Emma Cooper, a commissioning editor for documentaries at Channel 4. She thanked me for my comments, but said there was only so much detail that they could include in a 47-minute programme. She added that they chose the music they used because it was current at the time and apologised for any distress the programme had caused me.

She concluded by telling me that they would take my comments on board if they were to make a similar programme in the future, and wanted to assure me that the programme-makers did not set out to cause additional stress by discussing the events.

Yet again, it was a case of closing the stable door after the horse had bolted.

CHAPTER 51

REDUNDANCY

No sooner had I got through the stress of *Sexting Teachers* than I had another issue to deal with. The company I was working for was going through some big changes, introducing new procedures and technology, and I knew that there were inevitably going to be redundancies. In a way, my team and I were victims of our own success, as we had introduced the new systems that the company had implemented, and now our roles were no longer needed.

I knew I wasn't going to be there forever, but I was still sad about the idea of leaving. I'd been with the company for 10 years and they had been wonderful employers. During this time I had made some very close friends, including Chloe and Darcee, and of course it's where I met Paul. It had been a big part of my life.

Seven of us were called to a meeting in Milton Keynes and I was very anxious to hear what they had to say. I have always worked really hard to provide for my children and had worked my way up through the company, so it was going to be very strange to have this safety net taken away from under me. I never took the idea of redundancy personally, though. I know it can really knock some people's confidence, but I knew that I wasn't losing my job because of anything performance-related.

I was offered another job, but it would have meant even longer working hours, which would have meant even less time with the children. By this point I was working full-time again and didn't feel I was spending enough time with them as it was.

I looked carefully at the redundancy package being offered and discussed it with Paul, then decided to accept the offer. I knew it would mean stepping out into the unknown again and leaving behind the status, respect and earnings I'd been getting before, but it felt like the right thing to do and Paul's job was safe.

My boss was really supportive and looked at other options, but my mind was made up; I needed a bit of time out. Within a matter of weeks, I had packed up my pencil case and said my goodbyes …

CHAPTER 52

A NEW PROJECT

Throughout the trial and ever since, friends and family kept saying that I should write a book about what happened. So much rubbish has been written about what happened to Gemma and my family, and they were desperate for the truth to be told.

My family and friends know my opinions about speaking to the press and they all loyally kept their silence throughout the whole period. But equally, there were plenty of times when I would read something in the newspapers or hear somebody say something on the television and be itching to pick up the phone to tell them that they had got it all wrong. It was tempting, but I knew that kind of knee-jerk reaction wasn't the right way forward.

Since the trial finished, I had been concentrating on trying to hold down my job, keeping the family together and helping Gemma find a way through what had happened, so I just didn't have the head-space for anything else. But shortly after I was made redundant, yet another story about Gemma appeared in the press – this time talking about how many boyfriends she'd had since Forrest – and so I decided enough is enough, this needs to stop. Even after all this time, people were still discussing my family and putting two and two together and coming up with five; I'd just had enough.

I'm so proud of my kids and the dignity that they have shown throughout all of this. They could have gone and vented to the press, but they never did. But I was concerned that people were still discussing our lives, and would continue to do so unless I spoke out myself. So one day while I was at home, I was looking at my collection of biographies and started thinking, 'I wonder if I could do something like that?' I was always quite good at English at school and kept diaries, so I typed the words 'how to write a book' into Google.

I was a bit scared by the idea of agents and writing a synopsis and so on, so I just wrote to some publishers directly. I was a bit thrown when John Blake Publishing came back to me quickly with a positive response – to be honest, I would probably have dealt with a rejection better because something like this was completely out of my comfort zone.

But less than a week later, we had met up and I had a contract for this book.

Before I signed anything, I discussed it with my children and explained why I needed to write the whole story down. I stressed that it wasn't about Gemma, but my feelings as a mother.

Gemma understands why this book has been so important to me. Together we have come a long way in our relationship since she ran away, but I would never presume to speak on her behalf. She is a very private person and needs to deal with things in her own time and on her own terms. The only thing I can do for her is to be there for her whenever she needs me, on good days and bad days.

Early on, she and I put a strategy in place where I would say to her, 'Give me an emotion'. I was at such a loss as to how to handle the situation, it was my way of getting her to tell me how she was feeling without us having to get into some long, awkward discussion about every single thought going through her head. She would say things like, 'Annoyance, exhaustion, anger, frustration'. It really helped us both communicate when she first came back from France.

We have moved on from that now, but it is still very important for me to allow Gemma to tell her own story on her own terms. She is a child who is the victim of a sexual offence, and she has to learn how to get on with the rest of her life. And she is doing brilliantly. She has a lovely boyfriend whom we have welcomed into the family and she is really moving forward with her life.

Every so often, something will be written in the papers about what happened to Gemma and we will discuss it, but now it is more important for us all to try and get on with our lives.

There is no textbook on how to deal with a situation like ours. It has been like having to learn a whole new language. I have had to find out about arrest warrants, judicial processes, child safeguarding policy, aftercare for victims of grooming … the list goes on and on.

I will never be able to get over the guilt that I feel. I can't stop feeling like I'm the worst mum in the world for letting this happen to Gemma. From the moment I found out what had been going on, it has been like walking down a dark path, trying desperately to find a light and work out how to do the right thing by her.

Something good has to come out of all of this. I have an overwhelming desire to try and give something back after the wonderful way that people have helped me over the last couple of years. What happened to my family can happen to anyone, and I won't rest until I can do something positive about it.

We are not over it by any means, but we are in a good place.

AFTERWORD

Throughout this book, I have said time and time again that my family and I just want things to get back to normal. The truth of the matter is that for us life will never be normal again. Everything changed the moment that Jeremy Forrest stole my daughter from us, and we all have to live with this for the rest of our lives.

I will always be known as 'the mother of the Runaway Schoolgirl'. I have become so used to answering the same questions again and again that the answers practically roll off my tongue before the person finishes speaking. 'Is she back living with you?', 'Does she still love him?', 'How is she coping?', 'What is she doing now?'

I know that people are interested in Gemma for a number of different reasons. Most people genuinely care; some are curious about whether what was written in the press was accurate while others talk to me as if I'm some sort of celebrity.

I am a mum first and foremost, and I will always be. My children are my pride and joy; I love them unconditionally. I am not a celebrity, nor am I Mary Poppins. I'm not perfect and I know that I sometimes get things wrong. But anyone who meets my children always says what a joy they are, how polite, well-spoken and hardworking they are. They are intelligent and full of compassion. People tell me that they are a credit to me. As I live with the guilt and try to come to terms with what happened, this is what gets me through.

If you are still wondering whether Jeremy Forrest is a sex offender, or whether this is really a love story, ask yourself these questions:

What would you do if your fourteen-year-old daughter came home from school and said: 'Mum, guess what? I have a new boyfriend and he's my maths teacher.' Would you accept it?

How would you like the idea of your daughter receiving naked pictures of her teacher?

Would you be OK about sending your daughter off to school and having one of her teachers look at her in a sexual way, kissing her and treating her as their 'favourite'?

Would you accept your child being taken abroad without your consent, when you know that the person your child is with is unstable and is placing their life in danger?

Would you accept that your child has been made to lie, live on their nerves with immense stress, and harbour secrets that they have been told they cannot share?

Would you be happy to know that your child's teacher has been writing songs using words like 'heroin' to describe the feelings they have for them?

Would you be OK knowing that your child's teacher is

privately messaging them via social media without your knowledge and using sexual references?

Would you forgive the teacher who makes you believe that your child is 'a bit of a pain' and lies about your child, making you truly believe he is telling the truth? After all, he *is* the teacher.

If you answer no to these questions, then, like me, you will now understand that Jeremy Forrest is a sex offender and this was never a love story.

But if you answered yes to any of these questions, then you have a very different idea of parenting to me.

Support and advice
Barnardo's: www.barnardos.org.uk
Catch22: www.catch-22.org.uk
Enough Abuse: www.enoughabuseuk.com
NSPCC: www.nspcc.org.uk
SEE Changes: www.seechanges.org
The WISE project: www.sussexcentralymca.org.uk/
information_advice_support/_wise_project

ACKNOWLEDGEMENTS

My family and I have received incredible support throughout this nightmare. I would like to take this opportunity to thank the following people:

To Sussex Police and all those involved in Operation Oakwood, who worked so tirelessly to find my daughter and ensure her safe return: I know this case affected you deeply and impacted your lives in some way or another, and I would like to thank you all for the compassion you showed us. We were overwhelmed by your dedication, determination and care, and will always be grateful for what you did for us.

To DCI Mark Ling and DI Neil Ralph: I will always struggle to find the words to describe exactly what you did for my family and me. Nobody will ever know how committed you were. I know it took up every moment of every day and even impacted your own personal lives – not to mention the added pressure of the international media watching you. You put your heart and soul into bringing my daughter back safe, and I feel extremely proud. Thank you from the bottom of my heart.

To DCI Jason Tingley and DI Andy Harbour: 'Thank you' doesn't even begin to describe how much your help throughout this ordeal has meant to us. From appearing on national television for the first time to learning a whole new set of laws and language! Please accept this acknowledgement as some way to express how thankful we will always be for the care you have both shown us.

To DC Hannah Elmer and DC Jim Parkinson: You are the best family liaison officers we could ever have asked for.

I would also like to acknowledge the following Sussex Police officers: DI Colin Dowle, Owain Gower, DC Paul Semple, DC Darren Jones, DS Claire Gill, DC Graham Pawson and Nick Cloke. Although you were working endlessly behind the scenes, I hope you realise that I was aware of your commitment.

To Gatwick Police: Thank you for the hospitality and sensitivity you showed us.

To the services who supported and advised Sussex Police – Interpol, the Serious Organised Crime Unit, MI5, the Home Office and the French police force – I will always be indebted to you for the part you played in securing the safe return of my daughter.

To senior crown prosecutor Simon Ringrose: Thank you for your constant efforts to keep my daughter and family protected and to ensure that we reached the verdict we achieved.

To Richard Barton, QC: You were outstanding!

To Lewes Crown Court Witness Services: Thank you for all the support you gave to my daughter and me. You made an extremely difficult situation bearable.

ACKNOWLEDGEMENTS

To Alison Cummings: Without your quick thinking, and acting on your findings, I may not have my daughter back with me today. I will never be able to repay you, but I would like you to know how grateful I will always be.

To Sarah Spain, Lewes practice manager, child services: I know you will never accept an acknowledgement when I start reeling off the list of things you have done for my family and me, as you have always said 'it's all part of the service'. What you fail to see is the impact you have made; I dread to think where we would be if we didn't have you. From the endless advice, arranging additional support, putting up with me on good and bad days, and everything in between, thank you, Sarah. You have been amazing and I cannot thank you enough.

To Matt Dunkley, former director of child services East Sussex: Thank you for the instant understanding of what we were going through and your willingness to do whatever you could for us.

To Douglas Sinclair, head of child safeguarding East Sussex: Thank you for going over and above to understand the complex issues in unknown territory, and in turn explaining them to me. Thank you, too, for your honesty and for standing by my side to make sure that I was updated, aware of everything and had a voice that was listened to.

To Iain Luxford, head of media relations East Sussex: Thank you for your invaluable advice.

To Lucy Wooler of Eastbourne Borough Council and John Scrace of Wealden Council: Thank you for being sympathetic and considerate to our needs to start again.

To Gavin Meadows: Thank you for accepting HR as your new best friends, which allowed me to be where I needed to be. Your sensitivity, care, understanding and friendship will always mean so much – thanks, boss!

To Sue Marsh and the team at FLESS, Sue Dench, Lilly's nursery and Alfie's school: Thank you for restoring my faith in the education system and reassuring me that my children are receiving the best care and education.

To Steven Maryan: Thank you for managing the worldwide social media, working alongside the police and creating the only site we endorsed. You are a true professional and friend.

To the British media and all those who supported us via social media: Thank you for your continuous coverage and for keeping the story alive for Gemma to be found.

To the Sky Broadcasting Executive Team: Thank you for providing first-class customer service.

To Nicole Carmichael and Jonathan Bowman, without whom this book wouldn't have been possible: Thank you for your guidance and understanding of why this book is so important to me. I know it has taken up far more of your time than you ever expected, but the end result is very special. Thank you. x x x

To all my family and friends: I am so proud of your courage and the integrity you have shown, despite how tough the situation became. I would never have got through this without you all. You mean everything to me. I love you all! x x x